Wild Transformation

Matthew W. Morine

CYPRESS

Catalog in Publication

Morine, Matthew (Matthew Wayne), 1977-
Wild transformation / Matthew Morine
p. cm.
Includes scripture index.
1. Christian life I. Author. II. Title.
248.4 DDC21
ISBN: 978-1-956811-43-8 (pbk.) ; 978-1-956811-44-5 (ebook).
LCCN: 2023935644
Cover designed by Brad McKinnon and Brittany Vander Maas.

For more information:

Cypress Publications
PO Box HCU
3625 Helton Drive
Florence, AL 35630

www.hcu.edu/publications

Elders should not be bosses, but brothers.
This book is dedicated to Donald Moore.
He has been my friend and elder.

Acknowledgments

This book is my journey in Christ, but the journey would not be told completely without the numerous people who have crossed my path.

First, my wife, Charity. She is the most real Christian I know. Her transformational love for me is without measure. Every morning I find her reading her Bible, journaling, and praying. All that I have accomplished is because of her unbreakable character and commitment to our family. I know no greater human love than hers.

Second, my eldership and congregation. There are people who use and people who give. My eldership and congregation are truly givers. The organization that we are part of deeply influences us and having the blessing of being around such amazing elders and members has lifted my sails so that I could accomplish dreams that would not be imaginable without the support of my people. Also, the people I work with at Castle Rock church of Christ. Mark Walker, our other minister on staff is one of the finest men I know. He is more than a co-worker, he is a friend. I also have an amazing assistant, Pamela Kovarik. She is a joy to work with on a daily basis. To Gabrielle and Noah, you both have been a shining light to me. My deepest hope is for your transformation in Christ. You are so far in your journey and I could not be prouder of your progress. You both make me so proud.

Third, my mentors. God has provided amazing mentors to help me grow in Christ. Brian Garnett baptized me and helped me start my journey in Christ. Burnice Wesbrooks loved me during my formational days until he passed away. I cannot imagine my life without his gentle and supportive influence. Gregory Alan Tidwell continues to instruct me in the deep paths of wisdom. For being a simple midwestern preacher, his knowledge of all topics continues to astound me.

Fourth, Rianna Elmshaeuser helped with the editing and writing process. Also, Debra Wright helped with the final edits and Cypress Publications for publishing the book.

We cannot help to be a product of our culture. You take people away from a certain culture and put them into another place and much of what they are could be changed. The world that surrounds me is one of a rich blessing. The family I have and the people I am friends with are all part of the journey. Christ continues to providentially mold me through the people He puts into my world.

Contents

Wild Transformation

Foreword

Wild Transformation by Matthew Morine is an inspiring and transformative book that provides practical guidance and biblical content on living a Christian life with intentionality and purpose. The book covers a wide range of topics related to Christian living. It offers valuable insights for Christians of all ages and backgrounds.

The book begins by emphasizing the importance of action-driven Christianity, challenging readers to put their faith into practice and positively impact the world around them. From there, the book delves into the importance of connection and fellowship with other believers, encouraging readers to build relationships and support one another in their spiritual journeys.

Throughout the book, Matthew emphasizes the importance of conforming to the image of Jesus and following His example in our daily lives. He also explores the delicate balance between culture and faith, challenging readers to live out their faith in a world that is often hostile to it while remaining true to their Christian values and beliefs.

Another theme throughout the book is the importance of submitting to authority and respecting those in power over us. Matthew also explores the role of suffering in the Christian journey and how we can find meaning and purpose in our struggles.

Throughout the book, Matthew emphasizes the importance of striving for sanctity and purity in our lives, using our time, talent, and treasure for God's purposes, and being a light to the world. He also emphasizes the importance of reflecting and letting God into our lives, cultivating faith, hope, and love in our daily lives.

In every way, *Wild Transformation* is an incredibly valuable resource for Christians and congregations looking to deepen their understanding of what it means to live a Christian life. It offers practical guidance and biblical content on a wide range of topics related to Christian living, challenging readers to grow in their faith and transform their lives.

For individual readers, *Wild Transformation* is an excellent tool for personal study and reflection, providing valuable insights and guidance for those seeking to deepen their spiritual journey. For congregations, the book is an excellent resource for Bible classes and study groups, helping to build connections and support among church members.

From my perspective, *Wild Transformation* is a must-read for anyone seeking to live a more thoughtful and considered Christian life. The book is filled with practical guidance and biblical content that will inspire and challenge readers to grow in their faith and transform their lives, both individually and as part of a larger church community.

Gregory Alan Tidwell

Chapter 1

Convert

Action-Driven Christianity

As I walked to my childhood friend's home in Nova Scotia, I remembered the years I went to his house to pick up freshly squeezed cow's milk from the cinderblock basement in the Canadian winter cold. Six months after leaving to attend Preacher Training School in Dallas, Texas, I returned to this familiar house. It was New Year's Eve, 1998, and I was there for a party. But those six months had transformed me. The person attending that party was as starkly contrasted to who I was six months ago as a Texas winter is to a Canadian winter.

Imagine leaving secular society in Canada to be entirely immersed in a Bible Belt school of preaching. The school filled every day with classes about Abraham, Moses, and Paul. We studied books called Leviticus, Esther, and Deuteronomy; classic reading for people who were raised attending Bible class, listening to sermons, and having spiritual conversations, but I was counting my spiritual age in months, not years. These topics were as foreign to this Canadian as calculus and cowboy boots.

The calm, Canadian farmhouse I remembered was alive with activity. A group of partiers was outside sharing a joint. Upstairs, teens were drinking, smoking, and partying into the night. Drunk people, cigarette smoke, and flirty girls were the norm, not the exception. Even gunshots rang from outside as rowdy, intoxicated boys fired off twelve-gauge shotguns to mark the turning of the calendar from 1998 to 1999. What astonished me most was the long, enthusiastic kiss from my companion's girlfriend as we leaned against that frozen cellar block. She was ringing in the New Year with my lips instead of her boyfriend's. After the kiss, we rejoined the celebrations, making our way back across the house through a wasteland of beer bottles.

The whole house buzzed with slurred speech, staggering steps, and sin. Sin surrounded that home. Only seven months ago, all this was normal to me, but my time in Texas had created a new context. Learning to preach, praying to God, and studying the scriptures took the place of evil. On that New Year's Eve, the worldliness seemed so distant and strange for this preaching school student. For one more night, I watched the trappings of a former life.

In the back of my Bible, were the exact steps of salvation: Hear the gospel (Rom 10:17), believe the gospel (Mark 16:15–16), repent of sins (Acts 17:30), confess that Christ is Lord (Matt 10:32–33), and be baptized for the remission of sins (Acts 2:38) These were part of my mindset. My faith washed my sins away and I received the gift of the Holy Spirit, but here I was living like the rest of the world. That night showed me that I could be saved, yet still not purified. Jesus commands, "If anyone would come after me, let him deny himself and take up his cross daily and follow me" (Luke 9:23).

After twenty-two years of sobriety, I can boldly say that putting on Christ is the simple part of salvation. Taking up the cross and the daily aspects of salvation are the struggle. Being a disciple of Christ is infinitely more significant than the signing up process; true discipleship is transforming yourself into the image of Jesus. You give up the battle for personal independence and submit yourself to the rule of God. Jesus is the master, and you desire to do his will when you choose salvation.

Finding Transformation

Too often, Christians will lament their lack of transformation stories. Members of the church will say, "Matthew, I was raised in the church, and I have never known what it was like to be in the world," or "I do not have a powerful transformation story like you." These lines amaze me. Do people indeed not have a memory of bringing Christ into their lives? Somebody doesn't need to be pulled from alcoholism to see profound improvement throughout everyday life.

People raised with the lessons of Jesus may have had a head start in the spiritual realm; however, for those who have not seen a recognizable change in action and character, there is a critical step missing from their journey with God. How might lifelong members of the church ponder their existence without seeing spiritual improvement? Did these members always love others as Christ loves others perfectly? Have these members always been full of deep compassion? Do these members always speak with seasoned sweetness?

Underlining the lack of spiritual reflection is the assumption that converting to Christianity is merely about salvation, not transformation. No one in the church believes "once

saved, always saved," but when there is no identifiable transformation, the hidden mindset is "once saved, always safe."
True Christianity is about salvation and *sanctification*.

Everyone Has a Salvation Story

I was teaching some years ago about evangelism during an
online class and told my salvation story. I was demonstrating
the need to share the gospel through a story format instead of
a fact format. One student, who grew up in a Christian
family, had attended church his entire life, and was a faithful
Christian, worried he didn't have a transformational moment
to share with others looking to learn about Jesus. Part of the
story-sharing aspect I teach deals with starting your story by
sharing a weakness. This method involves building rapport
through confession of a defect, but this member felt like he
had nothing to contribute.

Think about this for a moment. What kind of image
did he have of himself and his family? Were he and his
family perfect, nothing ever dysfunctional, sinful, or
harmful growing up? Did he not have even one weakness
to confess to someone looking for Christ? Was there no
profound change in his character—with his tongue, his
conduct, or his affection? Was there nothing that he
needed to gain to be more in line with the image of Jesus
Christ? Nothing? This individual's far-from-unique
outlook astounded me because it seems to me that he had
not put much effort into finding spiritual transformation in
his life.

People who claim the "always Christian" status need to
look at the apostle Paul. He was a Pharisee, a lifelong
follower of God. However, when he put on Christ, he had a

passion for continued transformation. He gives his spiritual pedigree in Philippians 3:4–6:

> I myself have a reason for confidence in the flesh also. If anyone else thinks he has a reason for confidence in the flesh, I have more: circumcised on the eighth day, of the people of Israel, of the tribe of Benjamin, a Hebrew of Hebrews; as to the law, a Pharisee; as to zeal, a persecutor of the church; as to righteousness under the law, blameless.

Paul was a moral and upright person from his background. He followed God's laws and was passionate about his faith, but he realized that he still had much to learn as a disciple of Christ. He never claimed to have arrived at a completed destination with his spiritual maturity. He never stopped growing. He realized that to stop growing was a weakness and said, "Not that I have already obtained this or am already perfect, but I press on to make it my own because Christ Jesus has made me his own" (Phil 3:12). If Paul had to be intentional about spiritual formation, so should we.

The Role of the Church in Spiritual Revival

What I love about the Lord's church is the restoration spirit. We restored the plan of salvation. We must baptize people for the remission of their sins. People must believe that Jesus is Lord and confess his name. Everyone has to repent, so we must pay attention to change and ask ourselves if we are committed to heavenly change. Is there an apprenticeship intention in our gatherings? Individuals have consistently accused the congregation that "we baptize them, yet we don't teach them." People blame the church community and say that there is more focus on salvation than progressive sanctification.

Perhaps this thought process is because baptisms are easier to quantify. It's a public and outward event. You don't usually know when somebody has battled an internal struggle and won. You can keep a running count of baptisms for the year, but no one will take a picture of the man listening to his wife instead of yelling at her and posting it on social media. We celebrate baptisms because counting them is easier than quantifying spiritual progress. Measuring the increase of the fruit of the Spirit (Gal 5:22–23) is almost impossible.

Regardless if someone can measure it or not, the work of transformation is essential to Christianity. The journey of spiritual formation is wild, unpredictable, and untamable, a journey that is chaotic but vital to Christianity. Without character formation and without experiencing God's power of transformation, a Christian becomes stagnant. Little by little, transformation restores Christians to a full embodiment of Jesus Christ. Paul, keeping in touch with a gathering of battling Christians in Corinth, announced the objective of transformation:

> For the love of Christ controls us because we have concluded this: that one has died for all, therefore all have died; and he died for all, that those who live might no longer live for themselves but for him who for their sake died and was raised. From now on, therefore, we regard no one according to the flesh. Even though we once regarded Christ according to the flesh, we regard him

thus no longer. Therefore, if anyone is in Christ, he is a new creation. The old has passed away; behold, the new has come (2 Cor 5:14–17).

Further, Paul notes that the "love of Christ controls" him. The idea of control describes pressure that produces action.

The Purity of Love

Love is the pressure placed on our hearts. God used the death of Jesus as a vice grip on human souls to squeeze impurity out. Like a rag that has soaked up deadly sin, God applied pressure to remove toxic worldliness from our minds and dipped us into his love to soak up a new heart. We died to ourselves. We sacrificed the tyrannical self to allow the Savior to take our place. Paul words it this way in Galatians 2:20:

> I have been crucified with Christ. It is no longer I who live, but Christ who lives in me. And the life I now live in the flesh, I live by faith in the Son of God, who loved me and gave himself for me.

No matter the length of personal spiritual history, Christians are continuing to emerge as butterflies for God. The change is never finished because we must continue to transform throughout our lives. With salvation, the Christian is saved from sin, yet all through life that Christian is evolving. The cycle is moving one way or the other: away from Christ or nearer to Christ. No adherent of the faith is static. The Christian is being influenced by the material world or the divine reality. In verse 18, Paul uses the phrase "I might live to God," which indicates a past action with continuing results in the present. God plants new desires, loves, and inclinations in the heart. The old self's domination loses its grip on the heart because the pressure of the love of Christ drives out the desires of the flesh.

The new birth of conversion is instantaneous, but the process of sanctification is lifelong. Some people might be further along on the journey than those who did not grow up with spiritual teachings. Regardless of whether that person has come from a completely secular mindset or a spiritual mindset, the pathway of spiritual formation is the same. The wild process of transformation might be unpredictable, and full of ebbs and flows, but the endgame is to be as close to the image of Christ as possible. A Christian on a spiritual journey should be constantly increasing in the fruit of the Spirit. Love should flow from his or her heart. All should be transforming to have a gentle and kind nature.

Christians demonstrate a strong core of confrontation. If someone, after twenty-two years of being a Christian, cannot see spiritual improvement, then that person has missed the point of conversion. Salvation is more significant than a rescue from hell; instead, it is an invitation to be a new creation. God made the world and Adam and Eve, and when you are recreated to be in the image of Christ, like before, God pronounces that to be good.

Waking up from partying like it was 1999, I realized that it was not good. *Never again*, I said to myself. On that evening, my former self won out. All the advancement in Bible study didn't stop me from the wrongdoing that was so natural to me. Lying in a room in that cool cellar reminded me of the weak spot in my heart. I understood that change was more than one decision; it is a profound difference in your way of life. At that moment, I was not preparing for the Christian living struggles inherent to a fledgling faith, but the lifelong battle—that came with this revelation—would begin the very next day.

Questions

1. How could it bless us to remember—and even record—our own conversion story?
2. Are there any potential dangers as we share our conversion stories with others? Explain.
3. Is there biblical precedent for using one's conversion story to encourage others?
4. Explore the statement: "The new birth of conversion is instantaneous, but the process of sanctification is lifelong."
5. Why do some new Christians stagnate spiritually? What stops them in their tracks?

Chapter 2

Connection

The Christian Community and the Trinity

The Woodford family picked me up from my friend's house the morning after the party. As I made the melancholy walk to their family van, I left one community for another. My head pounding, my body aching, and my face haggard from the rough living, I climbed into the van and sat between eight-year-old Madison and six-year-old Rivera. The two sisters had black hair and bubbly personalities. Their cuteness came with normally endearing chatter but today it radiated like a jackhammer through my hungover head. I was in no shape to carry on a discussion, but the sisters never stopped for the remainder of the day. The Woodford family was picking me up to take me to my new community, the church's progressive supper.

Only church folks would come up with an event in which you would travel from the house of one hospitable saint to the next eating as a group. The first house serves an appetizer, the second house a soup or salad, the third house comes in with the soup or salad that wasn't served at the last house, while the fourth house provided a serving of meat or a main course. Depending on how many people signed up to serve, you might even eat another main course. The final site provides the dessert. By house three, your stomach is full to the point of discomfort and the rest of the houses are visited out of politeness. No one, and I mean no one, is still hungry by the dessert house, but who could turn down the sweets? After all, imagine the rich people on the Titanic waving off the dessert cart not knowing it was their last meal. Who knows what the future may hold! By the time everyone has hit all of the homes and stuffed themselves into their cars to drive home, the sin of gluttony has been maxed out and jokingly swept under the dining room table.

Now, take a hungover heathen, put him together with an overstuffed Christian and you get the vile version of me that day. I spent all day with the Christian community after spending all night with a partying community. The underlying personalities in these communities were not as different as you could hope for. People at the party were mostly pleasant, kind, and warm, while some were annoying, rude, and out of control. The Christians were mostly friendly, kind, and upbeat; however, some were blabbering, boring, and just plain exhausting. I would like to discuss how brilliant and lovely Christian individuals are compared to non-Christian individuals, but the truth is not all individuals who carry the Christian name are changed within. Therefore, there is little contrast between the types of behavior that people in the world have opposed to the behavior of those in the Word. Some individuals are fabulously centered around showing Christ, while others bring shame to His name with their appalling behavior.

Despite the similarities between the individuals in these two communities, worldly people and Christian people, I would choose the Christians every single time. People have cast off participation with a local congregation because of "the people." Sometimes it is not even all "the people" but rather "that person." One sour grape has ruined the entire progressive dinner! All this is to say that on the pathway to spiritual transformation, God uses all people. He uses them to shape you by the suffering they cause, or He uses them to mold you through love and nurturing.

The Role of Community in Transformation

The power of people on transformation is a wild experience. People are unpredictable and full of the whole gamut of emotions from unspeakable pain to near-perfect content- ment. A deep, meaningful relationship is life-giving, while a toxic relationship is soul-draining. Transformation comes from the connections we make in the church. Through time, relationships become progressively deeper, adding layers of accountability, heartbreak, and satisfaction. After years in the church, the people who will be remembered are those who treated me well or those who treated me poorly. On that fateful New Year's Day, God used two spirited little girls to punish me for drinking again. At the same time, I was inspired because I never wanted to be a disappointment to those who invested in me again. God uses people of all types to fashion us.

My spiritual journey as a Christian has been trying, especially that first year. After being baptized in Texas, returning home to do Christianity without the mission, and starting school in a distant city, I realized that without the care and concern of the Christian families within the Kentville Church of Christ, the likelihood of me being faithful today would have been greatly diminished. The Garnett family, the Woodford family, the Bearden family, and the Wisemen family all invested in my spiritual growth. During that time, I was attending the Nova Scotia Community College Halifax campus to train as a Heating, Air Conditioning, Refrigeration, and Ventilation worker. I remember Ray Wisemen driving more than an hour down to Halifax on a few occasions to attend the Wednesday night Bible study with me so I could get plugged into that group.

The general American attitude is one of independence, a Lone Ranger mindset. Countless self-made images are prevalent in pop culture:

- "I pulled *myself* up from my bootstraps."
- "I did it *my* way."
- "He is a *self-made* man."

These slogans are lies because all people need people. Even the Lone Ranger had Tonto.

The widespread idea of the wisest man in the world is usually an image of a priest or guru completely isolated on a remote pinnacle of a distant mountain. The implication is that profound improvement comes from sitting quietly on land devoid of people, and shrewdness comes from long periods of self-assessment. The glaring flaw in this belief is that with no one else around, there is only the self.

Self is at the center of this type of training. It is easy to be kind when there is only yourself to be kind to. Patience is long-lasting when there is no one testing it. Forgiveness is perfect when there is no one who has sinned against you. Holding your tongue and controlling your speech is simple when there is no one to speak to. Self-reflection, self-assessment, and solitude have their place but it is not what God wants for his children all the time.

Promoting Spiritual Change

There is time to allow for personal reflection, but an unhealthy fixation on your thoughts, feelings, and insights can descend into idolatry. Not the idolatry that worships a lion or an eagle made from wood or marble, but the idolatry of worship of the tyrannical self. The person focuses inward on the self when the inner self is full of deceit and self-delusion. People hear voices or feel nudges to do this or that and attribute all this spiritual direction to God when it is rooted in the ego.

No one can discern God's will for himself apart from the Bible, which is our source of insight from the Lord. God does not speak face-to-face to man but through the Word of God. God not only provides wisdom (Jas 1:5) through his Word but also through community. You can find the pathway of understanding through interactions with others. Everyone can feel wise or spiritually mature in a self-built echo chamber, but it is in community that you discover actual knowledge through associating with others and putting your thoughts to the test. Proverbs 18:17 says, "The one who states his case first seems right until the other comes and examines him." Imagine being the judge of your own conscience. That is precisely what people do with an isolated form of spiritual devotion. Self-reflection is wise up to a point, but it must be tempered through God's Word and God's people. God shapes people through people.

We are products of our connections in the Lord. Managing relationships in the church resembles training an untamed animal. One day the beast is quiet. The next day the beast rips into you without warning. Inside a congregation, there are many relationships, and an individual needs to explore them with care. Some relationships are life-satisfying because they resemble a favorite, well-worn T-shirt. You're used to them, and they provide high levels of comfort and functionality. Others are like a new pair of shoes. You have to walk awhile with them before they fit right.

A church is a field for spiritual improvement, and the different connections found there are reflected in your growth as a Christian. The combination of positive and negative social interactions helps refine your character like a stone tumbler. Sharp edges are smoothed, any dirt or ugliness is chipped off and washed away, and the beauty of the inner layers begins to shine through and sparkle. Change through connections is also disorderly. Through clash, caring, and concern, God forms the Christian character. There are times of extreme conflict, moments of life-sustaining love, and challenges of maintaining patience through the problems that refine a Christian like no other spiritual discipline.

Spreading Faithfulness Through Christians

The Hebrews writer appeals to the entire community to help Christians be faithful. The entire community is involved in the process of spirituality. Hebrews 10:24–25 says,

> And let us consider how we may spur one another on toward love and good deeds, not giving up meeting together, as some are in the habit of doing, but encour-

aging one another—and all the more as you see the Day approaching.

Some use these verses as a hammer to provoke guilt, while others argue that the verses are not speaking about Sunday morning worship. Either way, the verses do teach the principles of community influence.

Growing up, we had horses, and we used spurs, a metal point you drive into the horse's side, to motivate it to move. It hurts. People who believe that no one should ever be critical of them or harp on them for unchristian behavior have likely never ridden a horse. Sometimes people need a spur, or as people say in the South, "a kick in the backside." Our congregations probably have gone too far in the category of tolerance for skipping times together. Perhaps there was a time in which harsh preaching and judgmental spirits reigned in our churches, but the pendulum has swung too far the other way in our current culture. Being positive is the preferred option, but there is no such thing as a faithful Christian who is not connected to the church's head, and it is tough to be connected to the head while being separate from the body of Christ (Col 1:18).

Spiritual formation through community makes sense because the Godhead is a community. The triune Godhead is the model for discipleship. The Trinity is one of affirmation, support, and unity. God, throughout the gospel account, reaffirms how pleased He is in Jesus. During the Transfiguration, God announced He was well-pleased with His Son. Having a father edify a son is transformational. Repeatedly, Paul writes to the Corinthian congregation to build each other up. Seven times he implores them (1 Cor 8:1; 10:23; 14:4; 14:12; 14:26; 2 Cor 10:8; 13:10). Everybody presumably has encountered the moment in which a dad is disciplining his child in front of his friends. The child's head hangs down, his face is flushed, and his shoulders droop with disgrace. The kid is helpless—nobody hungers for a public dressing down. All people crave approval and a father's endorsement, even Jesus.

A group that is instructed on many occasions in sacred text to edify each other won't ever add up to much while individuals toss antagonism and venomous words at one another. Members will lament their leaders: the preachers stink, the deacons stink, and the elders stink. They say, "We need better leaders." They never stop to think that maybe it is not the leadership that is the problem but the hypercritical and downright unscriptural actions of members who refuse to be like God the Father. Paul declares,

> Rather, speaking the truth in love, we are to grow up in every way into him who is the head, into Christ, from whom the whole body, joined and held together by every joint with which it is equipped, when each part is working properly, makes the body grow so that it builds itself up in love (Eph 4:15–16).

Notice that an edifying congregation self-perpetuates, "it builds itself up in love."

On the other hand, a congregation that "bites and devours" each other tears itself apart. There is absolutely no way for a Christian to be spiritually formed by a critical church. It is ridiculous for people to think that a congregation is fighting amongst themselves to produce spiritually growing believers. A person who has been attacked by a grizzly bear would not become healed if he was not tended to after he was wounded. His or her exposed flesh would need to be cared for and the cuts bandaged before the body could function normally again.

The Power of the Trinity in the Community

The Trinity supports one another. Jesus endorses the mission of God, and the Holy Spirit supports the mission of Jesus. A transformational community is on board with a plan. The ugly head of individualism deforms the church because everyone is fighting for control over the congregation's mission. I would love to never hear again, "I do not agree with the direction of ... so we are leaving." Jesus was looking for what God was doing and got on board with the plan. There was no mystery meeting between the Holy Spirit and Jesus that excluded God. Individuals need allies, not haters.

A sound congregation bolsters one another because a sound congregation mimics the Godhead. You can see that support is part of the unity of a body. Too often people become so individualistic that there are fights over what the new floor in the auditorium should be and matters of opinion. People refuse to back one another in scriptural projections and plans. A new Christian expects Christian people to love each other. What a notion! It might sound trite, but love is always right. Paul summarizes this law in Romans 13:8–10. He states it fulfills the law through the love of the neighbor. You do not have to tell others to avoid stealing, adultery, and bitter battles because love for each other eliminates these destructive behaviors.

The Christian community should not only feed people with a potluck or a progressive dinner but the character and conduct of other Christians should nurture others' spiritual maturity as well. All Christians have the responsibility to stay connected to the church, and all Christians are responsible for helping each other grow together. Gatherings help take care of Christians because Christians cannot stand alone. Before we serve a physical dinner that will not create the development we are expecting, we should understand how to form deeper connections and feed one another spiritually.

Questions

1. Why does the Lord add those who are being saved to His church?
2. How does being an active church member bless and promote the process of spiritual transformation?
3. Think of a fellow Christian who has particularly blessed your spiritual growth. Specifically, how did they bless you?
4. Think of a young or struggling Christian whose spiritual journey you could bless. How can you best lean into this opportunity?
5. How does our knowledge of the Trinity boost our appreciation of healthy spiritual relationships?

Chapter 3

Conformed

Learning to Be Like Jesus

T he book cover had a bold, purple font with a glossy title on the front and a picture that kept my attention. The material in front of me was expertly crafted using graphic design principles to draw people in. The publishers were aiming to sell thousands of copies of this material. The problem was that at the school I was attending this material was frowned upon, and even having it would negatively affect me. Even though I could see no harm in the material I held in my hands, I concealed it from my roommate because I didn't want him to snitch on me. I hid it under my mattress until I could bring it out again in the evening.

People might not hide Christianity under a mattress, but too often, they keep it hidden from others or push it away from their consciousness. People have pushed Christianity into private realms rather than celebrating it with public and vocal expressions of faith. They might dust off their faith and bring it out in public on Sunday mornings, they may even read the Bible at home, but they are pressured to keep all religion out of the public square.

Now and then, some movement or slogan will take hold and bring Christianity out to the forefront for a time. For a while, WWJD (What Would Jesus Do?) bracelets were all the rage followed by a Jesus fish, also known as an ichthys, on the family car. But real transformation is more significant than slapping a sticker on your back window or a bracelet on your wrist. Those who only show their Christianity when it is popular and acceptable are missing a deeper trans-formation.

There is a massive difference between Christian "fan-dom" and spiritual transformation. For example, a fan will buy a Tennessee Volunteers hat, perhaps even a sweatshirt, and attend a game. These fans will showcase support for the team through what they display. If you drive down I-40 on a Saturday morning before game day, countless fans will have Volunteer flags waving out of their windows. People honk, wave, and feel great to be part of the team, even if it's just a small part. They all talk about how "we" beat Alabama or "we" almost got Florida this year, which inspires loyalty to the team. But loyalty is not transformation.

To really change and be part of the team would involve signing up to play for the University of Tennessee, attending team meetings, working in the weight room for hours, and sweating on the practice field doing drill after drill to perfect your game. There will be hours of game tapes watched, play-books studied, and feedback implemented. By the time all of that is done, the new team member would no longer be the same person inside or out. His body would be changed with added muscle and fitness. His mind would understand every aspect of the game including what plays the team runs and what plays their adversaries run. He would know his role and how to maximize his potential.

A person can be overweight, eat poorly, rarely touch a football, and be a fan of the team. But true players conform to the standards set by the coach and the team. They push themselves to be the best football player they can be. Too often, we have fans of Christ, not players. If there is no change, there is no discipleship, and people will engage in the fanfare of Christianity without engaging in the deeper, more disciplined aspects of being a follower of Christ. A fan can watch; a player transforms his body. Change is not about wearing a cross but carrying your cross daily.

Knowledge Alone Is Not Transformation

There is a transformation that happens to the player and the Christian, but not the fan.

> We are not like Moses, who would put a veil over his face to prevent the Israelites from seeing the end of what was passing away. But their minds were made dull, for to this day the same veil remains when the old covenant is read. It has not been removed because only in Christ is it taken away. Even to this day, when Moses is read, a veil covers their hearts. But whenever anyone turns to the Lord, the veil is taken away. Now the Lord is the Spirit, and where the Spirit of the Lord is, there is freedom. And we all, who with unveiled faces contemplate the Lord's glory, are being transformed into his image with ever-increasing glory, which comes from the Lord, who is the Spirit (2 Cor 3:13–18).

The opening verses in this passage allude to the law of

Moses. The listeners in Jesus's day would have been well-familiar with the Old Testament laws. Their way of life was an oral transmission model. Individuals didn't Google to search through Leviticus or look through books they kept at home. The role of memorization provided instruction and all the information would be kept in their heads, shared through the generations

Notice that complete knowledge of the rules and commands of God brought through Moses did not remove the veil over their hearts and reveal the nature of God. Doctrine, orders, and facts *about* the gospel are not the gospel. Information is not transformation. Knowledge of Christ is not a replacement for modeling our lives after Jesus Christ. Would someone who has every command in the Bible memorized but has never heard of Jesus be a Christian? How about a person who could list the Ten Commandants and has never eaten unclean food? Or someone who partakes in the Lord's Supper, attends every Sunday, and goes through all the correct motions? A person could do all of that, but if he or she was not demonstrating the character of Christ, that is not Christian behavior.

Rules do not automatically lead to a transformed life. The believers in Corinth could follow all the rules of Moses and still be hiding true Christianity from the community. Second Corinthians 3:14–15 says,

> But their minds were hardened. For to this day, when they read the old covenant, that same veil remains unlifted, because only through Christ is it taken away. Yes, to this day, whenever Moses is read, a veil lies over their hearts.

Jesus unveils the transformed life.

The Relationships of Knowledge and Action

Years ago, I was playing Ping-Pong with a professor. The game was intense, and my teacher, Avon Malone, was using the game to mentor me. He asked me about a recent test I took to graduate from the school I was attending at that time. This test drilled me about my views on marriage, divorce, and remarriage, my idea of how the Holy Spirit worked, what I thought about instrumental music, women's roles, and even hand clapping. The questions dealt with every minute detail of correct doctrine. There is no shame in being doctrinally right. The Bible indeed teaches the truth about an assortment of areas. After telling Mr. Malone about the questions on the test, he stopped and looked at me. Then he asked, "Did it ask you if you believe that Jesus Christ is the Christ?"

My answer was a simple, "No." I could have passed the test, graduated from that school, and gone on to live a life devoid of Christ. I could never have found out that my loyalty and model for living was Jesus. All the doctrine could have been right, but what does that matter if my life was out of alignment with the Lord? If I could critique the Lord's church, I would say we have placed divine law above Christlike living. We have allowed ourselves to succumb to a checklist of Christianity. There is nothing wrong with all the lists that we have created, but lists of rules do not transform. They do not "lift the veil" from our hearts. All through school, I was trained to spit back a list of facts on a test—memorize the list, take the test, write down the list—but in no way does my ability to regenerate that list mean that I was transformed from the knowledge I held.

Paul states in 1 Corinthians 8:1, "Now concerning food offered to idols: we know that 'all of us possess knowledge.' This 'knowledge' puffs up, but love builds up." He continues to define the insidious nature of knowledge that can lead to false pride in 1 Corinthians 13:1–2:

> If I speak in the tongues of men and angels, but have not love, I am a noisy gong or a clanging cymbal. And if I have prophetic powers, and understand all mysteries and all knowledge, and if I have all faith, so as to remove mountains, but have not to love, I am nothing.

Then, in verses 4–8, he elaborates on the true nature of love. An individual can perform spectacular demonstrations of strictness and piety, yet without a groundbreaking adoration of Christ and others, that individual is pushy and annoying, not cherishing and nourishing.

We have the five steps of salvation, however, you could do these acts and still be off base. Your body performed them; however, your heart was not in them. There was no feeling or devotion, just checking items off a list. That is not the life Christ called us to.

Reflecting the Image of Christ

We are called to conform to the image of Christ. Second Corinthians 3:18 says,

> And we all, with unveiled face, beholding the glory of the Lord, are being transformed into the same image from

one degree of glory to another. For this comes from the
Lord who is the Spirit.

The idea of being conformed means that someone has
pressed the image of Christ onto us. You have been placed in
a mold, and pressure and time have reshaped your being. At
first, you were like a square of hardened clay trying to fit
through a circular hole. But God is using time, circum-
stances, and people in your life to soften you up and carve
away the elements of your character that are at odds with the
nature of Christ.

This process can be painful and put you under tremendous pressure. You probably fought it because of your innate
sense of self. You wanted to be you, not someone else. But
with time, the individualistic spirit is softened and replaced
with submission. The self was crucified to make room for
Christ. God has one goal for you. It is not for you to have a
happy life nor for you to get only yourself to heaven. He is
persistent in his goal to transform you into his Son; for your
benefit and the benefit of those around you.

All Christians following Jesus are being conformed to
His image. A Christian takes on the likeness of Jesus. The
divinity of Christ focuses on the divine nature of Jesus, but
Jesus was also fully a man like all of us. He worked as a
carpenter, carrying on business, dealing with demanding
customers, and probably even hitting his thumb with the
hammer now and then.

James, the brother of Jesus, wrote a book about the
applicable code of conduct. He talked about controlling the
tongue, counting it all joy during suffering, and being fair to
all people regardless of clothing and cash, and all of this was
what he saw Jesus do before he became famous. He

witnessed Jesus paying attention to the most impoverished customer. He probably watched Jesus being chewed out by a client and holding his tongue.

Jesus is divine, but He was also a tradesman during the first century in a Jewish community. When people think about being like Jesus, they have lofty expectations perhaps of teaching large crowds and getting a lot of attention. The Lord's glory is also in everyday kindnesses, love, and courtesies extended to all people. Your face might not shine with the glory of the Lord like Moses, but your life will shine with the love of Christ through your treatment of others. The concept is not complicated. First Peter 1:16 explains it well, "be holy, for I am holy."

The Spirit is at work within Christians to facilitate this transformation. All Christians are becoming more aligned with either the ways of the Spirit or the ways of the material world. Romans 8:5–6 says,

> For those who live according to the flesh set their minds on the things of the flesh, but those who live according to the Spirit set their minds on the things of the Spirit. For to set the mind on the flesh is death, but to set the mind on the Spirit is life and peace.

The future is bright for Christianity. It can transform Christians into the image of Christ, which shines ever more radiantly within a dark world. A light in the darkness has a powerful impact. As Christians, the culture is attempting to put a filter over Christians that lowers the intensity of their light, but the light of love coming from true image-bearers of Christ is powerful and draws people in. America's culture is entwined with Christianity. However, a divide has begun in the culture, and the split is getting more extensive. As the gap increases, a Christian being transformed into the image of Jesus will stick out. Now is the perfect opportunity to be that pure and unfiltered light. Remove the veil and let your light shine.

We are to be image-bearers of Jesus. That was what I wanted to be while I was at school. So, at night, I would reach under my mattress and pull out the book called *Just Like Jesus* by Max Lucado. The book was frowned upon at my school because Max said and taught some wrong things. While it is true he is wrong about some things, at that point in my walk with the Lord, I was craving to know what Jesus was like, and this book seemed to provide some answers.

Doctrine is essential, but there is so much more to the faith. Transformation is the goal, not just knowledge. I needed change, and I needed to be just like Jesus. Being just like Jesus is the call of God. However, within this pursuit, we can easily miss the point of salvation, discipleship, and church. My main issue was that I still had no clue who Jesus was, so I began studying to find out more. This thirst to know Jesus personally was the next step as I continued my path of spiritual discovery.

Questions

1. Why must knowing Jesus be THE goal of our spiritual growth?
2. Why is more than just factual knowledge needed for spiritual transformation?
3. Why is spiritual transformation such demanding work?

4. How does it help us to know that Jesus faced every type and category of temptation that we face?

5. Of all the trials and temptations faced by Jesus, which do you consider most challenging? Why?

Chapter 4

Culture

Balancing Culture and Faith

I walked out of the country-and-western store decked out in black cowboy boots with a stitched pattern on the side and a cowboy hat perched on my head. The straw hat was bent to perfection as I walked toward the Garnett family doing my best impression of a Texan. It was my first time in Texas. Unfortunately, my gait was a little uncertain because the slippery sole of my new boots had a higher heel than this Canadian was used to. But what really made my imitation of a cowboy evident was obvious for all to see: I was missing the number one component of a cowboy—not a barrel chest, nor sun-damaged skin, nor the bow-legged walk of a man more comfortable on a horse than on his own legs. No, the number one sign that I was not a true Texas cowboy was my lack of a belt buckle.

All true cowboys have an ornately rounded piece of gold-plated jewelry flashing in the sun, drawing attention with its grandeur. The bigger the buckle, the better the cowboy. For reasons unknown, I missed this cornerstone of a cowboy's look in my attempt to blend in. Rather than being a genuine man from Texas, I was a wannabe kid from Nova Scotia. I knew more about lighthouses than I did about riding a quarter horse across an open field. I was unable to wrangle cows, yet I could land a solid halibut. I may have been attempting to blend into the Texas culture, but my actual culture was obvious. I never did achieve that Texas cowboy look. I may have gotten duded up to be one with a big hat and stylish boots, but I was a fraud.

This same problem happens all too often with Christians who have become part of the broader culture. Instead of standing out as a light of a different culture, they blend into the world. Everyone has seen examples of Christians mimicking the world. But even more deadly is when Christians are blind to how culture has shaped them. As far as this believer is concerned, he or she is standing out for Christ's mission, and his or her values are infused with the Spirit. In reality, media, culture, and politics have formed them more than the Word of God. This kind of Christian is like a Midwesterner claiming to be a Southerner when he doesn't have an accent. He can't hear himself because he thinks that he has the perfect voice for what he claims to be. He defines Christianity through his own example. "I am a Christian, so everything I do and think is what a Christian is." With this mindset, culture replaces Christianity, and the people of God redefine godly living through the filter of the world.

Culture and the Church Clashing

What is the right way to deal with cultural influence in the church? Typically, there are two responses to the culture within the church. One is to reject it entirely, and the other is to embrace the culture. One answer turns the church into an outdated, imprisoned organization that rarely connects to the world. People no longer see believers as people full of joy but as people wearing denim and riding in buggies who have no relevance to the life that people are living. Then again, the church sometimes adjusts to culture so much that it loses most of what distinguishes it from popular culture.

Social change warriors rage against the seemingly out-of-date ethical practices in the belief that their expanded acknowledgment of cultural practices will connect with the world because a feeling of "coolness" will return. Unfortunately, the two scenarios create a similar response from non-believers—what's the point of messing with the church? It is either so out of touch it's pointless to join or it is so "in touch" there is no reason to join because it is no different than their current life. Individuals believe that the congregation is "futile" or without "reason."

Christians live in conflict because we are attempting to find the proper balance between living in the world and being separate from the world. The Bible talks about Christians not being of the world. John 15:19 states, "If you were of the world, the world would love its own; but because you are not of the world, but I chose you out of the world, therefore, the world hates you." There is a gap between the standards of the world and the ideals of Christians. On the other hand, the Bible teaches Christians to live in the present world. Matthew 5:14 commands, "You are the light of the world." Paul implored the Corinthians not to reject association with all the unrighteous people in the world "since then you would need to go out of the world" (1 Cor 5:10). These verses that teach separation and attachment to the world lead us back to the familiar slogan "in the world but not of the world." But this slogan is easier said than lived. There is constant conflict within Christians to discover the balance in becoming a "peculiar people" (Titus 2:14).

Finding Balance Between Culture and the Church

The history of the churches of Christ bears out this struggle of locating the proper balance between living in two worlds. Many Restoration leaders were against getting entangled with the affairs of this world. In David Lipscomb's book *Civil Government*, he argues against Christians even voting. There was also a strong sense of pacifism in the Restoration Movement. Christians were encouraged to avoid the current political affairs of the world. But as time elapsed, this anti-world basis began to shift to a stance that embraced using our rights as citizens to influence the world around us. Now young Christians are encouraged to seek positions that can persuade others to embrace Christian values, and it is desirable for Christians to hold political offices in government despite the church's history of emphasizing the standard of living counter-culturally versus embedding ourselves in the culture.

Since this conflict of living with the "elementary principles of the world" and maintaining our "heavenly citizenship" is a constant concern to grapple with, how can we live in balance with these seemingly contradictory principles (Col 2:20; Phil 3:20)? There are two realms Christians must maintain harmony with to fulfill God's desire for us to be "in the world but not of the world."

Inside the church, there is by all accounts a vibe that Christians are above culture. It resembles the fish that doesn't understand he is swimming in water. Indeed, even

Jesus was cognizant of the culture. He was a Jewish man brought into the world in a normal town and had parents. He was born during a period in which the Romans were ruling the known world. He communicated and spoke the language of that time. Jesus fit into his culture in a way that allowed him to connect to people, yet he also conducted himself according to God's laws, rather than man's. He lived in the world, but how he treated others and interacted with the community was not defined by the current culture.

Picture Jesus if He ignored the way of life around Him. Instead, He wore shorts, and a backward cap, and pulled out His iPhone to check the climate. Rather than discussing sheep and sand, He discussed PCs and Facebook and used words like "dude" and "groovy." All these instances would not have made sense to the people He lived with, but that is all culture. Jesus would never have spoken English, and He certainly did not use the King James Version of the Bible. Instead, He used language and examples relevant to the culture.

What can happen to Christians is either over-adaptation or under-adaption. Over-adaptation is when Christians seek to connect to the culture instead of being a counter-cultural example. When non-believers look at the church they see more of the world rather than a cross-shaped community. The church allows sin into the body much like the Corinthians did, believing that loving the brother in sin for committing fornication was the best behavior (1 Cor 6). Instead of allowing culture to shape the church with the belief that changing will increase numbers or generate acceptance, the church must strive to set itself apart as unique. The world needs to see something different in the church than they do every other organization, or else why bother with Christianity if there is nothing distinct to mark it as different from any other belief system?

On the other hand, churches that under-adapt to culture become old-fashioned and irrelevant. People walk into the community of believers and wonder where the time machine is because these believers are not living in the current age. The automatic assumption is that these people have nothing to add of substance to a person's life. People come to them looking for answers and culturally irrelevant Christians do not give the impression of insight and wisdom. You would not ask an eighty-five-year-old to work your iPad, and you would not expect a seventy-five-year-old farmer to set up your Wi-Fi. These judgments might be ageism, but people are looking for information from sources they can trust. A long denim-skirted woman who hasn't had a haircut in fifteen years and who wears no make-up or jewelry would not be the go-to person for a teen girl struggling with high school peer pressure. First impressions count, and the church must be aware of the impact of those impressions.

Balancing culture and Christianity is essential. No one is above culture, and everyone is influenced by culture. A Christian must navigate through the wild and stormy seas of culture with wisdom and patience. Veering to either side will cause either compromise or complacency. Paul gives some pertinent advice to the Christians in Rome when he implores them to allow the influence of Christ to shape them more than the world around them.

> I appeal to you, therefore, brothers, by the mercies of God, to present your bodies as a living sacrifice, holy and acceptable to God, which is your spiritual worship. Do not be conformed to this world, but be transformed by the

renewal of your mind, that by testing you may discern
what is the will of God, what is good and acceptable and
perfect (Rom 12:1–2).

To fight against the pull of culture, a Christian has to
know his or her identity in Christ. A Christian isn't a captive
to culture but rather a captive to Christ. The strain between
the world's critical factors and the requirement for following
Christ will fight for God's children's personalities. Paul
makes another polarity. He discussed being a slave to righteousness or a captive to sin. He implores his listeners not to
be conformed to the world but to be transformed by Christ.
The transformation occurs in the mind of an individual,
which moves out into it the body. The brain controls the
conduct.

Continuing to Renew Your Christian Faith

Renewing the mind is a lifelong process. Jesus asked His
audience about John's baptism. He created the polarity of
whether His baptism was from heaven or man.

Jesus answered them,

> "I also will ask you one question, and if you tell me the
> answer, then I also will tell you by what authority I do
> these things. The baptism of John, from where did it
> come? From heaven or from man?" And they discussed it
> among themselves, saying, "If we say, 'From heaven,' he
> will say to us, 'Why then did you not believe him?' But if
> we say, 'From man,' we are afraid of the crowd, for they
> all hold that John was a prophet" (Matt 21:24–26).

The way that Jesus deals with this question is how all Christians should deal with cultural issues. Is there express truth forbidding a practice? If yes, the course followed is wrong and will be unsuitable for the entirety of time, but much of what people think is the truth is culture. People believe that regulating behavior or actions will provide real transformation, but notice that in Romans 12:2 change happens in the mind. People can argue incessantly about modern behavior such as the style of dress or type of music, but all actions should use God's guidance. Does this behavior come from a place of godliness in mind or from a place of rebellion?

The soul makes an activity significant. Paul needed to find a way into the culture to win others to Christ (1 Cor 9:20). What is the inspiration for the conduct? A more profound shift of the heart needs to happen because Christians have tossed out godly conduct repeatedly in favor of imposing their cultural norms on those of a different culture. For example, an older person will unabashedly scold a teenage girl on the way she dresses while wearing fifty thousand dollars worth of jewelry (1 Tim 2:9). Perhaps the teenage girl is dressed inappropriately, but the older lady cannot see past her culture and has neglected to speak to her sister in Christ in love. People turn on one another because of cultural differences, fail to love their neighbor as themselves and miss the real issue. What is happening in people's hearts and minds? Transformation starts in the mind and then informs culture.

Connection Matters

As Christians, we have to connect to culture as much as we fight against it. I remember being a minister in the small town of Waynesboro, Tennessee. There were about 2,000 people in the whole town. One afternoon, my wife looked at me and said, "You are the best Canadian redneck I have ever seen." She was referring to my enthusiasm for Tennessee Volunteers football, my attendance at all the high school games, and my love of barbeque. I got into what the people of the town enjoyed. There was nothing sinful in my new hobbies, and they helped the townspeople relate to me better and gave us something to talk about. And it worked both ways. While I lived there, more than a few citizens mysteriously developed an interest in hockey.

My transformation into a "Canadian redneck" was not instant and took some adjustment from both sides. The biggest culture shock moment came when I hosted a trip to a Nashville Predators game. There was a fight between two players during the game, and I jumped up and shouted, "No one wins until there is blood!" Fighting is part of the game for a Canadian hockey fan, but all the church members looked at me with judging eyes. How dare their minister yell this. Years later, one of the girls, now grown, who had attended that game told me the story from the Tennessee point of view. She included how everyone in the church thought I was terrible for cheering on a fight. What was interesting was that she and her family became big hockey fans after that. She laughed as she said, "Now we jump up and yell 'no one wins until there is blood.'" Now as a more seasoned minister, I can see how my bloodlust may not have been quite as Christlike as it should have been. Transformation starts in the mind, but we have to protect ourselves against becoming blind to the impact of culture on our hearts and minds.

Questions

1. How can we become more consistently aware of both the positive and the negative impacts of culture on our spiritual growth?
2. Why is it wise to seek such awareness?
3. In what ways can we properly use our understanding of culture to move others toward Jesus?
4. How might unwise Christians misuse culture in their evangelistic efforts?
5. To what extent should we be culturally tolerant? What are the biblical limitations?

Chapter 5

Submission

Submitting to the Powers that Be

No two Christian couples are the same in the world. Every relationship has specific distinguishing characteristics. Some Christian couples are so overly affectionate that they make others around them uncomfortable, while other couples are rarely seen to touch in public. Some couples are playful and others can only conjure up a half of a smile between them.

Blending two personalities in a marriage creates a wide variety of pairs. Some couples are equal partners, and in other couples one person clearly dominates. One interesting couple I watched proclaimed a highly traditional structure of authority. The wife was always talking about how submissive she was to her husband and how he was her head, her Lord, her chief. She would go on and on preaching her view of the biblical verses covering wifely submission. She would lecture women in class about a wife's need to be submissive to her husband using herself as an example of how her man was in charge of the home and her spiritual life. However, I learned from her that years ago the couple had agreed that she would make all the little decisions for the family and her husband would make all the big decisions. Interestingly, it just so happened that in all their years of marriage, there had never been any big decisions to make for their household! She made all the calls for the family. She gloried and boasted in her submission while never submitting to anyone.

How People Resist Submission

The role of submission in spiritual transformation has nearly disappeared in American church culture. One of the reasons is that, like the woman above, everybody believes they are submissive until the time arrives to be submissive. When they are called upon to submit, there is always a reason or excuse that relieves them of the responsibility to submit. You hear it everywhere.

- "I would do what the boss says, but he has no clue what he is doing."
- "I would submit to my husband, but he is a selfish man."
- "I would listen to my seniors, yet one of them tends to drink too much, and I won't follow a man who does that."

Rather than surrendering a specific measure of control, we have become specialists in submission avoidance. People are experts at finding a way to excuse their behavior. This would be like the clay rejecting the guiding hand of the potter, remaining a lump of dirt instead of being shaped into something beautiful with a purpose.

The person who fights against authority and refuses to

submit rejects the shaping artistry of God. God allows people to leave him, but their consequence is staying as a formless, useless clump of clay instead of being fashioned by God. The refusal to submit to others is a rejection that pushes God away and declares that man's ability to shape himself is better than God's. Instead of a spiritually enriched person, an idol of stubborn pride is formed in the individual's heart. The reality is man's skill is nothing compared to God's. People who choose the uncompromising path and reject God's molding in spiritual formation turn out like a five-year-old's Play-Doh figurine instead of Michelangelo's David statue.

Submission Is Biblical

Scrolling through the Bible is a wake-up call for submission. Look at all the commands for requests in the various relationships.

- Let every person be subject to the governing authorities. For there is no authority except from God, and those that exist have been instituted by God (Rom 13:1).
- For the mind that is set on the flesh is hostile to God, for it does not submit to God's law; indeed, it cannot (Rom 8:7).
- [Submit] to one another out of reverence for Christ (Eph 5:21).
- Wives, submit to your husbands, as to the Lord (Eph 5:22).

- Now as the church submits to Christ, so also wives should submit in everything to their husbands (Eph 5:24).
- Obey your leaders and submit to them, for they are keeping watch over your souls, as those who will have to give an account. Let them do this with joy and not with groaning, for that would be of no advantage to you (Heb 13:17).
- Be subject for the Lord's sake to every human institution, whether it be to the emperor as supreme ... (1 Pet 2:13).

Look at all the areas that Christians are ordered to submit or be subject to someone. Christians are to submit to the public authority, to God's law, to each other, to spouses, to Christ, to the older members, to the church leaders, and even to go so far as to try to submit to the pagan sovereigns of Rome. In a world that is brimming with the conversation of the individual's "privileges and rights," the Bible is filled with instructions for individuals to submit to others and so be satisfying to God.

The message in the Bible is to submit. The lesson in the world is to exert authority. Think about the heroes of our culture. There are very few statues of people who submitted to authorities. George Washington did not become a hero for accepting taxation without representation. Even Martin Luther King Jr., who led peaceful protests, still stood up to Jim Crow laws' authority within the land. Rather than complacently moving to the rear of the bus and complying, Rosa Parks split with convention and sat in the front. America is brimming with legends who stood firmly in opposition to oppressive guidelines. So where is the harmony between an individual assertion of rights and submission to authority? Our culture has gone from one individual refusing to move to the back of a bus sending a message of equal treatment to individuals robbing Rolex stores in New York City proclaiming the same message for the sake of progress.

Culture Resists Spiritual Submission

The undercurrent of America is one of gaining power, privilege, and living life on your terms. The idea is to stand up, speak up, and stop the system of oppression. A bold sense of "no one will tell me what to do" controls people's perspectives. There is undoubtedly a time to say, "Enough is enough," but the general writing of the Bible is a command for submission. The focus on compliance is so great that even Paul commands slaves to be obedient to their masters:

> Bondservants, obey your earthly masters with fear and trembling, with a sincere heart, as you would Christ, not by way of eye-service, as people-pleasers, but as bondservants of Christ, doing the will of God from the heart, rendering service with a good will as to the Lord and not to man, knowing that whatever good anyone does, this he will receive back from the Lord, whether he is a bondservant or is free (Eph 6:5–8).

Thus, the principle of submission is so rooted in a Christian way of life that Paul said it is better to be submissive to a person who would own you than to rebel against their authority. Considering all these verses and lessons on submission, the go-to for Christians should be submission, not defiance. There should be a straightforward scriptural explanation behind somebody intentionally dismissing authority rather than the flimsy excuses that are frequently given for not submitting.

Submission Within the Church

As the years progressed, the fights inside churches were regularly fueled by discussions about who ought to submit to whom. The practice of submission can be misused by leaders *and* members. Both sides stop fighting about who needs to give in to the other party. The focus often turns to discussing the weak and healthy in the congregation (1 Cor 8). One side argues that the other side needs to submit to them because of biblical command or the offending of the conscience, while the other side might say that he or she is in authority and the people need to submit to them.

Sometimes the issue is foolish. On one occasion, I saw some members fighting about opening the doors at the back of the hall. Yes, the debate was about whether the doors in the back should be open or shut. One side expressed that the entryways being closed established an ideal love climate, and those individuals are entitled to their opinion. The other side held that the doors ought to be open because others are to remain in the back and watch from the corridor. It was a clinical issue because the individuals needed to stand up during the meeting. Each side had its reasons for wanting the doors to be open or shut. Each side boisterously argued its point. Both used the instruction of "submit one to another" to advocate for the other to submit to them. Rather than practicing the scripture themselves, they demanded the other party was out of line. The submission principle was used as a hammer to beat the other party.

Negative interactions with Christians have defeated the desire for the people of God to be submissive to one another. The problem is that self-will reigns more than the concept of mutual submission in our congregations. The world will use authority to control others, and sometimes all there is for a Christian to do is be peaceable in the midst of conflict. The point remains that as believers, domineering is unacceptable behavior. Peter cautions elders from lording over the flock (1 Pet 5:3). Paul warns masters to stop threatening slaves (Eph 6:9). All Christians are to practice mutual submission no matter what their station in life is (Eph 5:21).

The appeal to submit is rooted in one's submission to God and scripture. In all the above scriptures, the motivation comes from one's love for Christ. Do not submit with a resistant heart that merely outwardly complies but instead submit with an inward basis of being pleasing to God. If Christians will not submit to God and His commands and will not listen to scripture, there is no way possible that they will be formed into the image of Jesus Christ. Reject the molding work of God and scripture and there is little hope for transformation. This principle is borne out in people who come to church for decades and no one has ever seen spiritual growth within. They might have been practicing the sin of self-will all along.

How Submission Should Work

The model for submission is Jesus Christ. Philippians 2:6–8 is a classic text on the concept of compliance.

Who, though he was in the form of God, did not count equality with God a thing to be grasped, but emptied himself, by taking the form of a servant, being born in the likeness of men. And being found in human form, he humbled himself by becoming obedient to the point of death, even death on a cross.

With that in mind, Christ, who had all authority and position of power willingly sacrificed it to die for humanity, is a testament to how far humans should go in the act of submission. Of course, there is a line that can be crossed because of the corrupt nature of humanity's authority, but that line in the sand is probably further back than most Christians would feel comfortable. The bar is closer to personal self-destruction than to individual freedoms. Jesus denied His sense of privilege to be a sin offering for humanity.

Even when Christ fulfilled his mission and all authority was given to Him, He voluntarily relinquished His Father's power. The best example of mutual submission is found within the Godhead.

For "God has put all things in subjection under his feet." But when it says, "all things are put in subjection," it is plain that he is excepted who put all things in subjection under him. When all things are subjected to him, then the Son himself will also be subjected to him who put all things in subjection under him, that God may be all in all (1 Cor 15:27–28).

First Corinthians 15:24–27 emphasizes the post-resurrection work of Jesus, wherein he overthrows the present age's rule and authority. Toward the end of time, Jesus Christ will rule until He has stifled the entirety of God's adversaries and obliterated each malevolent ruler, power, force, sin, and death. The inestimable fight will end with His triumph; however, the critical point lives in His complete submission. Jesus will give up the entirety of His natural force and authority to carry brilliance to God the Father. Christ won't commit insubordination, a typical propensity for men in power positions, yet will deny His supreme force to pay tribute to God.

The Glory of Submission

The instinct of man is to increase personal power, not submit to another's authority. This habit all too often creates a decrease in submissive obedience and weakness in faith. The importance of independence in modern society promotes pride and an unwillingness to be submissive to anything, even God. Hebrews 5:8–9 states, "Although he was a son, he learned obedience through what he suffered. And being made perfect, he became the source of eternal salvation to all who obey him." We need to remember Christ's example: as His authority increased, so did His submissive obedience. He never abused His authority to escape persecution or death but instead revealed the impermanence of earthly power through humility and subservience to God.

The idea of "all in all" is that Jesus acts so that God is glorified, not Himself. His submission to His Father is for the Father's pleasure and benefit. Christ has been given all the world to rule, and He turns it over to His Father. These verses are a divine example of the nature of mutual submission. Both parties are quick to give authority to the other member of the Godhead. Instead of war for power, there is humility in submitting to one another. At the core is the desire to want what is best for the other person and not oneself. It is called self-denial.

Questions

1. Why do most people in our broader culture view 'submission" as a negative word?
2. What impresses you most about Jesus's practice of submission?
3. Besides Jesus, what other biblical examples of godly submission impress you?
4. In what ways does the practice of godly submission bless us?
5. What is the glory—the virtue, the impact, the shining crown—of submission?

Chapter 6

Wild Transformation

Suffering

T hrough the years, I have taken a lot of kids and teens to climb mountains. A mountain trip includes waking up in the middle of the night, typically around 2 or 3 a.m. You start a two-hour drive from Denver into the mountains to arrive at the trailhead at approximately 5 a.m. The sky is dark, and the air is cold and crisp, almost crackling like frost. The instant you step out of the warm car into the brisk mountain air, your breath makes a cloud as you scramble to put on your jacket, warm beanie, and gloves. Invigorated by the cold, you set out on a long walk up to the mountaintop.

Over the years, I have noticed a critical element between those who summit and those who turn back before the goal is reached. One would think that this element would be physical fitness, that the people in better shape would be the successful summiteers, but that is not the case. I have seen six-year-olds stand at the top while highly fit sixteen-year-olds give up before the top. A person's fitness and strength have little to do with predicting success. My friend said it best when he defined the critical element this way, "Summitting is about how much suffering you can take." When your legs burn, your lungs ache, and you've grown bored of walking past countless trees and rocks for endless miles, that is where the separation occurs between the victorious summiteers and those who are going for a long walk back to the car with no victory to share.

How much suffering can you take? Maybe this principle of enduring suffering applies to Christians. What makes the difference between a believer on earth who gives up and someone who makes it to the heavenly reward? What is the core element that separates those who fall away and those who keep the faith? There is almost a disconnect between American Christianity and biblical examples of faith.

- Abram left home to follow the call of God.
- Joseph went to prison for his beliefs.
- Paul traveled thousands of miles to share the gospel and was beaten over and over again for his faith.

Jesus promises His disciples that they will suffer, but American Christians have a laundry list of gripes. Our churches have become a spot in which members whine about the song tempo and become annoyed about the auditorium being excessively cold or warm throughout the late spring. Individuals have left assemblies because somebody was discourteous to them. Our congregations have become delicate. We are more worried about comfort than change. Nobody is happy to be inconvenienced during worship service. What would happen if real persecution came? Would we endure it for the sake of the gospel?

What Suffering Does for Christians

What is funny is people will genuinely argue the point that persecution is worse today than in the past. People will assert that the government is opposed to Christianity, the community does not respect the church like before, or that teens are tempted more today than in days past. How can they honestly believe that? When was the last time a parent watched his or her spouse or child being thrown into jail for their faith? Or the last time their church service was interrupted by government officials with guns, and we haven't heard about it.

The reality is in America today people are not beaten by leaders for confessing Christ. Victimhood has become our national currency, and the church doesn't want to miss out on this status-gaining category. People try to be a victim in this world because they have not developed true faith and have missed the point. We have had it so good for so long that we are looking for persecution and define mild discrimination as such. Today we have to search out and exaggerate to find an example of persecution. In the first century, they did not have to look; pain found them. Our churches are full of people who never had to make the gut-wrenching decision to follow Christ and suffer or deny Him and be set free. Suffering breaks you or molds you.

In the book *Make Your Bed* by William McRaven, a Navy SEAL, talks about the training program that all future SEALS endure. At the start of one class, there were 150 recruits. By the end, only 33 remained. Think about those original recruits; not one of these people was out of shape or weak-minded. To even be considered for a SEAL cadet took tremendous effort and being the best of the best. None of these men came into the program as couch potatoes or video game addicts. All of them would have been in the best shape of their lives. No one was lazy, unmotivated, or inept. The distinction between the successful cadets and the lesser cadets was the capacity to endure suffering. The ones who could run into the icy sea and stay until near death, the ones who could be canvassed in mud and sand for hours, and those who had the mindset to never give up were transformed into SEALS. The change from sailors to some of the most elite warriors in the world happened as a result of enduring misery.

James, the brother of Jesus, makes the same point about suffering-producing character.

> Count it all joy, my brothers, when you meet trials of various kinds, for you know that the testing of your faith produces steadfastness. And let steadfastness have its full effect, that you may be perfect and complete, lacking in nothing (Jas 1:2–4).

James' advice in the twenty-first-century mindset is shockingly absent. Instead of complaining when people mock you at work or when you are not invited to parties because of your spiritual convictions, or worse yet, instead of calling up the elders to air your thoughts and grievances about what is going poorly in the church, maybe you should take a breath and count it all joy. After all, James was giving this command to those being sawed in two and fed to lions. Surely we can count it all joy when life becomes uncomfortable and inconvenient. When life treats you poorly, see it as an opportunity to create a robust faith and a genuine nature. The two words that James uses are "perfect" and "complete."

These words could also mean "mature." It is the idea of a completed project or transformation. There is no way possible for Christians to be like Christ without traveling on the road of suffering. Unless you are willing to take up your cross, you are not ready to be what Jesus is. There is no Christ without the suffering of the cross.

A radical call must sound forth from the church. Will you suffer for Christ? The call to discipleship is greater than coming to church, giving a little each week, and even reading the Bible daily. All of these actions are good and necessary, but what makes these actions transformational is the element of suffering. Suffering allows the Bible to be formational. It is more significant than inspiration, and it is the metal that suffering hammers on to mold it. Look back in history and find a leader who did not suffer. All great men and women had to pass through the crucible of fire to find themselves standing firmly on the other side of pain. The lessons learned empowered them for the coming journey.

Suffering in the Bible

Look at the list of verses that mention suffering in the Bible. Suffering is rarely discussed in the modern church, but it was a core teaching of the early church.

- For it has been granted to you that for the sake of Christ you should not only believe in him but also suffer for his sake (Phil 1:29).
- Share in suffering as a good soldier of Christ Jesus (2 Tim 2:3).
- Do not fear what you are about to suffer. Behold, the devil is about to throw some of you into

prison, that you may be tested, and for ten days you will have tribulation. Be faithful unto death, and I will give you the crown of life (Rev 2:10).

- This is evidence of the righteous judgment of God, that you may be considered worthy of the kingdom of God, for which you are also suffering (2 Thess 1:5).

The New Testament discusses languishing as an ordinary reality for a Christian, not a snapshot of distress or a briefly troublesome season. Instead, it is an expected occurrence for those living a dedicated life to Christ. I recollect years prior when a speaker said, "If you are not suffering as a Christian, maybe you are not living like a Christian." That may be valid or it may not be, yet suffering is expected in the Bible to be a significant part of a Christian's life.

The reason that suffering is so transformational is that Christ suffered for us. Christ was willing to suffer for the benefit of humanity. As Christians, we suffer for God. First Peter 2:20–24 preaches this vital point.

For what credit is it if, when you sin and are beaten for it, you endure? But if when you do good and suffer for it you endure, this is a gracious thing in the sight of God. For to this you have been called, because Christ also suffered for you, leaving you an example so that you might follow in his steps. He did not sin, and neither was deceit found in his mouth. When he was reviled, he did not revile in return; when he suffered, he did not threaten, but continued entrusting himself to him who judges justly. He himself bore our sins in his body on the tree, that we might die to sin and live to righteousness. By his wounds you have been healed.

Peter notes the injustice of suffering for your faith. Someone who sins and suffers because of it, that is expected. But the modern Christian has little expectation and understanding of suffering for Christ despite Peter's warning. One indication of this mindset that God will protect them from suffering is seeing book titles such as *Why God Lets Terrible Things Happen to Great Individuals*. Books with similar titles are prevalent. People also tend to believe that you will avoid a great deal of suffering by not bringing it on yourself through corrupt activities and instead living righteously for Christ. But these things do not shield you from suffering. The Christians in Peter's letter are being mistreated for their faith, and Peter is encouraging them. But he is not promising them an end to their affliction, rather he reminds them of Christ's perseverance and the healing that brought to all mankind. Christ endured, and Christians will as well.

There is causality that people tend to believe is behind suffering. They believe good people should not suffer. Even Job's friends of long ago had the human tendency to equate suffering with sinning. But that is simply not true. Look at all the injustices in Christ's story. He did not sin, and there was no deceit found in Him. He bore our sins, and He was wounded for us. By the modern standard, Christ, who lived a sinless life, should not have suffered, but He did. Good people suffer, but that suffering can cause good people to grow into even better people.

A Cultural Connection to Suffering

Look at the story of Theodore Roosevelt. He was an up-and-coming politician in the state of New York, but on one heartbreaking day in 1884, he lost his wife and mother within a twelve-hour period. His father had passed away a few years before. He was devastated. He quit all of his public work and traveled west to the Dakota Territory where he ranched for six years. When he left New York, he was somewhat of a sickly kid who had grown into somewhat of a sickly man. But he transformed himself into a barrel-chested, deep-voiced cowboy in those Badlands, and when he returned to New York in 1887, he was an imposing figure.

His time away transformed his character and his body from a boy to a man. He is the only president to actually lead men into battle. He formed the famous "Rough Riders" of the Spanish-American War. He could handle the trials of public office because he was intimately familiar with suffering. Suffering makes you stronger.

Suffering Allows You to Be Better

Suffering also makes you compassionate. Yes, you read that correctly. Suffering creates endurance, perseverance, and strength, but it also tenderizes the heart. The ability to empathize with others comes from your own sleepless nights of internal pain. Watching others suffer is unbearable, especially when they are children. People who have not suffered tremendous pain can be unpleasant and hurtful even when their intentions are good. However, individuals who have been in a deep pit of agony have crawled out of the hole to once again see the light, and come to the side of individuals who are suffering. Wounds seldom produce shortcomings. The injuries of Christ created a High Priest who had sympathy for His people. Hebrews 4:15 reads,

> For we do not have a high priest who is unable to sympathize with our weaknesses, but one who in every respect has been tempted as we are, yet without sin.

Jesus enduring unjust suffering is an encouragement because He went through the ordeal of the cross for Christians, not so we could explain why suffering exists, but so you can bear up under the suffering because He knows our pain. Jesus is not asking us to do something He was not willing to do Himself. Pain is a harsh master, but as modern Christians, there are some lessons that only suffering can teach. Too often, Christians avoid the lessons at the cost of their faith. Instead of growing more robust and becoming more mature through trials and suffering for their faith, modern Christians look for the easiest path. The only way to the summit is through suffering, by walking the valley of the shadow of death. We can walk boldly because Jesus walked there already for us.

Questions

1. Why do so many within our broader culture equate suffering with God's displeasure?
2. Give the numerous biblical examples to the contrary, why do many still teach that true Christians don't suffer?

3. What makes faithful suffering such a strong source of spiritual formation? Why does enduring suffering so profoundly shape us?
4. How can a Christian learn to find joy in suffering?
5. In what ways can we better support fellow Christians who are suffering? Non-Christian friends who are suffering?

Chapter 7

Sanctified

The Parts that Lead to Sanctity

The car was a vibrant Christmas red with tinted black windows on all sides which frequently vibrated with the booming bass beats of the latest rap music. That 1984 Mercury Cougar was outfitted with two 450-watt subwoofers in the trunk and a custom-made box to ensure no one escaped the sounds of my favorite songs. My car was worth $4,750; $4,000 of that value came from the stereo system. I had a tradition of hopping in my stereo-carrying car and driving to my cousin's each year to stay with him to attend the Bridgewater Exhibition, a Canadian fair.

My 1999 trip was particularly significant because I had just returned from Texas where I had been baptized to renounce my sins. I was full of new vigor for Christianity and excited to tell my cousin all about it. On the way there I picked up two teenage hitchhikers. I can't imagine what they were thinking as I rolled up in what appeared to be a drug dealer's vehicle. Maybe they were just thrilled to be picked up by someone like them or maybe they thought about declining the ride rather than riding in my rolling contradiction. There are a few oxymorons regarding Christians such as a Christian stripper or a Christian conman. I'm not saying what type of car Christians should drive, but maybe being driven by a recently stamped Christian in a car like mine fell into that category.

The two hitchhikers accepted the ride in the end and chatted a lot. The conversations centered on partying, drinking, and doing drugs. I hid it well, but I felt awkward in that situation because for weeks I had been in Texas surrounded by Christian culture. At church camp, no one talked about an acid trip or how good the weed was. Camp conversations centered around how singing 728B in a large gathering gives you goosebumps.

Being back in my old life, I realized the tone had shifted. My passengers glorified sin. As a new Christian, I could feel tension nipping at me. How could something so familiar feel so foreign? The answer is simple: I was a new creature. The old Matthew had died to sin and the new Matthew was trying to live for Christ. But, oh, how I wanted to fit in. My newfound energy for Christ had fled. I had no desire to give a rousing lesson on the destructive power of sin in this world and certainly did not want to start piping gospel music through my top-of-the-line sound system.

On the day of my baptism, my heart was on fire for Christ. For weeks, all I wanted to do was read the Bible and share Jesus, but as soon as those teens jumped into the car, I became mute. What a strange feeling it was—wanting the acceptance of two teens I had just met and who were dependent on me for a ride to the Bridgewater Exhibition. What started as a Christian duty—helping strangers—turned into me compromising my walk with God. I was not the Good Samaritan helping the bloodied man in the ditch nor the priest who strolled by on the opposite side. I was much worse. I turned into a man who helped the robbers and beat the helpless, guiltless soul rather than walking in the image of Christ. I resembled the youngsters. I became so easily lost, and I was driving too far from Christ.

Being Set Apart

On that day, the reality of walking with Christ really set in. Confession with Christ at church camp and being Christian there was easy. Walking with Christ in the world was the real challenge. Being sanctified in a world of sin takes some wild transformation. Thus, Christian formation is essential. Do you look like the world or do you look like the image of Christ? Do you appear to be like everyone else or do you stand out because of your commitment to Christ? These questions are the basic meaning of sanctification: "to be set apart." This concept goes back to the items used in the temple to serve the Lord in worship. Because these items were used to worship God, they could not be used for everyday, mundane purposes. Being used by God is a special privilege, and the things that were used in service to God by the priests had to be cleaned. Then how do we get from ancient Jewish temple items to the concept of "sanctified humans"?

Within the church, there is a heavy focus on baptism and being saved. That is the moment in which a person is saved and is given the Holy Spirit; his or her sins are washed away and that person becomes sanctified (Acts 2:38). In the sight of the Lord, they have been washed with the blood of Christ (Rom 6:3–4), and God views them through the lens of Christ's holiness. God has adopted the individual as a child. They now have positional sanctification, which means that they are freed from the *penalty* of sin at some past point. Ephesians 2:8 states, "I have been saved." At this point, the person is saved and is set apart for God.

Positional sanctification is about a moment in time. As long as the individual continues to walk in the light, the blood of Jesus covers continued sinful occurrences (1 John 1:5–10). Numerous Christians embrace this type of holiness, but God wants his people to continue to *progressive sanctification*. Too often, Christians treat spiritual growth like brushing crooked and rotten teeth. It's a good habit to get into, but without braces and dental work, nothing will get any better. They go through the motions without purposeful intentions.

Salvation and Spiritual Formation

Our spiritual formation is a partnership with God. The shift moves from salvation and the penalty of sin to deliverance from the *power* of sin. James notes, "Therefore put away all filthiness and rampant wickedness and receive with meekness the implanted word, which is able to save your souls" (Jas 1:21). A Christian continues to mature as God's child. God wants his children to be progressively changed (1 Thess 4:1–3). Some people put all spiritual transformation on God; it is His job to complete His work within us. Other people take a legalistic approach in which transformation is treated like a self-improvement project. But there is a balance between our activity and God's activity. God is forming us as we seek to develop ourselves. Both are in this process together. Paul notes,

Therefore, my beloved, as you have always obeyed, so now, not only as in my presence but much more in my absence, work out your salvation with fear and trembling, for it is God who works in you, both to will and to work for his good pleasure (Phil 2:12–13).

Scissors: A Metaphor for God and Man

C.S. Lewis used the image of scissors to illustrate the relationship between God and man. One needs both the top shear and bottom shear to cut a piece of paper. The scissors cannot fight over which side is most valuable. Both of them need to partner with one another to cut the paper—together. Progressive sanctification has God carrying the majority of the weight in the relationship. Still, without human motivation and energy for the goal, nothing is accomplished. God cannot and will not transform an unwilling heart for He refuses to override free will in salvation and sanctification.

Perfective Sanctification: The Ideal State

The final type of sanctification is perfective, which is the idea of salvation from the *presence* of sin. Paul notes, "I will be saved" (1 Thess. 5:9). At this level we find the final salvation of the soul and removal from a corrupted world. A Christian is perfected in Christ and has received that promised glorification. All Christians are striving for this final state.

God is doing everything He can to get you to the point of perfected sanctification. God will put people through suffering, pain, disappointment, anger, testing, blessing, community, whatever it takes to see you to the end saved (1 Tim

2:4). To get to the final state of salvation, God must make people holy. God is sacred, and to be like God, a person has to be like his or her Creator.

The issue inside the church is the absence of other-worldly change. As the years have progressed, I have seen life-long individuals from a church be some of the coldest, most horrible, profoundly unspiritual individuals. One has to remember that just showing up to a hospital does not automatically heal a person. Being in the right building does not mean you are right with God.

Christians can go to church every time the doors are open, read the Bible daily, and be consistent in their prayer, yet that heavenly transformation has never occurred. Why do individuals battle with change? I trust it is because we have become so acclimated to the traditions of Christians that we have lost our sense of wonder that we can be with God, the Creator of everything! Rather than delighting in our salvation and our freedom from the heavy burdens of sin, the church turns into another obligation, one more task to be completed before we get to heaven.

- Do we understand that love is standing before the God of the universe to praise Him, or do we battle with keeping the focus on the lesson or singing?
- When someone reads the Bible, do we realize that God Almighty is speaking to us, to humankind, or has it become a habit?
- Where is the sense of holy reverence for being in the presence of God?

The church has created rules and guidelines, not holiness. To experience supernatural, wild transformation, it is essential to restore a sense of awe and wonder at coming into the presence of the Lord again. When the early church met together, notice that the feeling was one of a sense of awe (Acts 2:43). Going through the motions will not transform you. Remembering the great God we serve and injecting a sense of wonder into our spiritual practices is where the reshaping of our souls begins.

Gaps in Holiness

When I was driving those hitchhiking teens, they were cursing and swearing. What shocked me was that I joined them. I wanted to fit in, not stand out. I liked the teen's affirmation more than God's respect. I did not want to be set apart from them. When they ultimately got out of the car and I continued driving, the crushing weight of guilt pressed down on my heart. "Wow, what did I just do?" I asked myself. I chose to please those random strangers over being acceptable to God. For the first time after becoming a new Christian, I felt the sting of sin and the need for repentance. What a failure I was. For a wild transformation to happen, a person has to push against culture. Perhaps in the past, the general culture was distinctly Christian but in today's world, Satan's forces have worked hard to remove the presence of God and any form of godliness from society.

Hope in Corinthians

We are all going to fail, and none of us will measure up to being perfect like Jesus, but that does not mean we stop trying. Everyone comes from a different background, but these verses in 1 Corinthians 6:9–11 give us all hope.

> Or do you not know that the unrighteous will not inherit the kingdom of God? Do not be deceived: neither the sexually immoral, nor idolaters, nor adulterers, nor men who practice homosexuality, nor thieves, nor the greedy, nor drunkards, nor revilers, nor swindlers will inherit the kingdom of God. And such were some of you. But you were washed, you were sanctified, you were justified in the name of the Lord Jesus Christ and by the Spirit of our God.

The list is pretty heavy and was given by Paul about some of the congregation members in Corinth. Imagine all these people walking into worship on Sunday morning today. There might be more than a few heads turned. But what I love about these verses is the line, "such were some of you." It seems the majority of church members were sexually immoral, adulterers, homosexuals, were greedy, but no longer because these individuals were transformed. God did his work in the hearts of these Christians by washing them and sanctifying them. All of the transformations happened with the convert's intentionality and the power of the Spirit of our God.

People read about the changes in the Corinthian congregation and rejoice, but have we thought about how the process took place? Do we believe that these sins magically disappeared overnight? Do we believe they all repented, were baptized, and their ways of life were changed in a flash? Most likely not, because they were humans just like us and that isn't how individuals change today nor for the rest of human history. The congregation needed to help each other walk with the individuals who were battling these sins. The greedy were not made the deacon over the finances. The previous homosexuals were not placed in positions of responsibility for the young men's outdoor trips.

We read about the change, yet I wager the process of change was lengthy with individuals coaching each other, having a program to help the individuals battling with each wrongdoing, and watching the everyday, steady work of transformation. Change is wild; there could be a long time of consistent improvement with one evening of complete relapse and failure that prompts a contrite heart that thought convinces them to repent and improve. For people to change, everyone is involved. Christians supporting Christians, God working through the Spirit, and the person's individual work and desire for change all join to form stories of transformation. No one element is more important than the next.

Christians Joining for Progress

Someone, not me, could have the most excellent car, get it all washed and cleaned, jump in for a road trip, and get nowhere. Why? Because without gas, the car doesn't run. It is stuck. Some progress could be made without the gas. Perhaps it could be pushed down a hill or even on a flat road, but all progress would stall out at the first hill. You need gas to make any significant progress. But if you have a can of gas and no car, that is worthless too. You need the car, the tires, and the engine to make progress. Everything has to come together to accomplish progress, and the church is a better place when all the parts work together. Our churches need to be filled with more stories of transformation. People need to see God working within us in unexpected ways to change the people who come to Him. The greatest joy is when we see people become like Christ before our eyes. We have a part to play; the Spirit is working, and the individual has to work too. When it all comes together, it is beautiful. But the story doesn't start unless we begin with the ideas in the next chapter.

Questions

1. How does Satan oppose the process of sanctification? What tricks, tools, and teachings does he use?
2. Besides the devil's opposition, what makes the process of sanctification so challenging?
3. If we fully embraced the process of sanctification, what would that look like? What wouldwe be doing better, more often, or not at all?
4. The goal of sanctification is _____.
5. Why does God give us such an important role in our sanctification?

Chapter 8

Sin

Depravity Has a Sneaky Nature

Ask any tourist to Colorado about viewing a mountain landscape, and that person will mention seeing mountain goats. Part of driving through Rocky Mountain National Park usually involves a roadblock at some point because of the people who have left their cars on the side of the road to get a picture of a dusty white mountain goat. Even Colorado natives love mountain goats. Everyone wants a photo of them and with them. People well up with happiness and satisfaction in their hearts when a few goats come meandering by and later tell the story to their friends when they return home. Traffic stops for the typical goat, which is poorly groomed and matted, but now and then a bright white-coated goat comes walking by, and all of the people go crazy like a teenage girl at whatever boy band concert is popular that week. The goats in return love human contact because of the food that people provide. A little trail mix or a few salty peanuts are the equivalents of a nice steak dinner for these goats.

Everyone loves mountain goats . . . but me. I hate them.

Yes, you read that correctly. I hate mountain goats. Saying this out loud to another person makes them react as if I've just said I don't believe babies are cute or that I don't care for bacon. I am aware I stand alone in this opinion, but I stand by it. While everyone else is surrounding the cute mountain goats, I stay in the car disgusted by them. I do not like looking at them, and I certainly do not want to take a picture with them. If I were going to look at them in any capacity, it would be through the scope of my rifle. After I shot them, I would take the carcass home, make goat jerky, and feed it to the dogs.

Before we get to the reason for my distaste of these loathsome creatures, I'd like to draw a comparison between the goats and sin. I believe mountain goats are from the devil just like sin is from the devil. Everyone loves mountain goats because they are cute and fluffy and make for a nice picture, but people do not see how damaging these savages are in real life.

Now, look at all of the pictures of sin in this world. The drinking images are of young people having a fantastic time with one another at a social gathering. Pretty women are hanging off the arm of a man with a six-pack of abs, and the people are smiling with beers in their hands. What is never shown are the negative consequences of drunkenness.

In Las Vegas, the billboards show off young women inviting men to see them for a good time. The women look happy and beautiful. According to the appealing lady on the billboard who seems eager to take her garments off for cash, there isn't any reason not to engage in such behaviors. The billboard plays up the idea that it's satisfying to deal in sin, but the beautiful woman on the billboard doesn't show the true spiritual ugliness of such behaviors. The fun and appealing side of transgressions is shown to lure people in. But there is a lot more to the story.

The Cloak of Sin

Sin is always cloaked. But behind the cloak is the family that is destroyed because of alcoholism. There are no magazine ads of the man who has beaten his wife and kids because he was intoxicated. They don't show images during the Super Bowl of the woman who drunkenly careened into the car of a young dad and his kindergarten twins in the backseat; he will never walk again because she had too many glasses of wine.

All of the people who have sexual diseases are never advertised nor are the hordes of men who have broken marriages and kids they rarely see. The suicide rates of sex workers are never pictured next to the smiling girls on the signs who have had the pain in their eyes photoshopped out. Even luxury car commercials show a smiling man but not what he has sacrificed to afford the car and all of the trappings of wealth; his family, marriage, and a sense of real emotional contentment.

Of course, sin is always pictured in a positive light for if it weren't, people wouldn't engage in it. Sin is the gold veneer on a lampstand—all flash, no substance. Sin is the fake autograph, the knockoff watch, and the counterfeit bill. The appearance is impressive, but the worth is artificial. People who fall prey to sin have been lured in by the pleasing presentation without having the wisdom to realize that some things are too good to be true.

People who desire real wild transformation must be able to recognize the evil mountain goat for what it is. Nothing halts the change into the image of Christ more than sin. Sin sabotages the spiritual growth process. The problem is that underneath the cloak of sin, evil grows in the soul instead of holiness. As long as people struggle with habitual sin and fail to see it for what it is, the sin pushes out the space created for spiritual transformation. Until they get past the enticing picture of sin and see the truth, the person will continue fighting a battle against evil to such an extent that the Spirit has little room to operate because it is fighting off the toxic poison that sin creates in the mind. The person cannot make leaps in Christian maturity because sin keeps the person in a perpetual spiritual battle for the heart and mind.

The Wisdom of James

James, the brother of Jesus, warns of the encompassing nature of sin.

> But each person is tempted when he is lured and enticed by his own desire. Then desire when it has conceived gives birth to sin, and sin, when it is fully grown, brings forth death (Jas 1:14–15).

James provides the life cycle for sin in these short verses.

The first stage of corruption is temptation. James is warning his readers that temptation starts in the heart and casting blame on others or situations doesn't allow one to take personal responsibility for their own actions. Too often, people want to blame their behavior on others. He or she was tired or it was the influence of the individuals around them which made them act that way. Adam accused Eve and even God of his sins.

Rather than searching for something to fault, James puts the weight of enticement on the Christian who has done wrong. What begins the principal phase of wrongdoing is one's own cravings. The picture of sin is appealing and captivating. The phrase "is tempted" is in the present tense in the original language, which underscores that temptation is continuing, and repeated, as well as the ever-present reality of fighting against the forces of Satan.

The idea of luring and enticing goes back to fishing imagery. Fish do not chomp on a lure the instant it's in the water. They check it out, swim around it, and watch it. The lure looks good and smells good. The fish takes a little nibble at the lure. Then, when that little nibble tastes good, the fish loses all caution and strikes, devouring it whole. Satan uses bait on people just like the fisherman uses on fish. He uses the right bait for the right fish that has an appeal that is too attractive for them to resist. Even though they've been warned about the hook, the lust of the flesh causes the person to rationalize away the consequences and justify the behavior— no one will know, no one will be hurt, and no damage will be done. They toy with it in their mind rather than swimming away.

The second stage of the lifecycle of sin is the sin itself. The temptation has ruminated within the mind long enough that the person acts upon it. Jesus warns of the power of the mind to conceive evil. He warns that both murder and adultery start in the mind (Matt 5:21–22, 27–28). The battle against sin is waged in the mind. God has provided some defenses against corruption like the conscience, which is the soul's early warning system. It gives us the ability to recognize that something is wrong with this tasty morsel just floating in the water; perhaps I should swim away. God has provided humans with feelings of guilt and morality to protect against the onset of sin, but sometimes the power of lusting after sin becomes too strong, and evil is brought to fruition. The fish disregards the hook which will lead to tremendous pain. And once you are hooked, it becomes exponentially more difficult to be free of the sin than it would have been to just swim away when something seemed wrong. Life will never be the same.

Fighting Sin

There are real strategies to fight against the power of sin and the first step to sabotage the life cycle of sin is self-reflection. You have to be aware of temptation and the temptation most attractive to you. Why is this thought or behavior enticing to you? What is happening in your life that is making the sin appealing? To stop the temptation process, the person has to be conscious of the devious thoughts being planted in their mind. The second way to stop the spread of sin in your mind is through accountability. The temptation is strong. Your desires can overwhelm the mind's internal defenses and cloud your judgment, so there is a need for someone from an outside perspective to provide feedback on your behavior. The lust of the flesh, eyes, and the pride of life all conspire to lead people into sin, but having an honest and wise person give feedback can wake up the conned Christian. The mind plays tricks on the heart but having someone willing to talk some sense into the mind is so helpful. At the point when an individual's own inner voice has been deceived and broken down a Christian's good standing, a faithful companion can give the warning of a threat. The third means to stop the life-cycle of sin is to eliminate the temptation. The psyche will harp on sin and the more that you ponder a specific activity or enticement, the harder to resist it will become and will expand until it's all you can think about.

The Bible discusses fleeing sin because being within sight of the enticement is overpowering. Joseph needed to run from the advances of Potiphar's wife. In discussing greed, Paul advises Timothy to escape from the love for wealth by supplanting the desire with the pursuit of godliness and righteousness. First Timothy 6:11 says, "But as for you, O man of God, flee these things. Pursue righteousness, godliness, faith, love, steadfastness, gentleness." People think that through the force of will, a person can overcome the lust of sin, but over and over again, in the Bible, the advice is to replace evil with godly living. Paul tells the thief to do more than stop stealing. He commands him to be productive in providing for others. Ephesians 4:28 says, "Let the thief no longer steal, but rather let him labor, doing honest work with his own hands, so that he may have something to share with anyone in need."

Satan's Lure

We need successful strategies to deal with sin because Satan is looking to destroy us by luring us into a bad habit or a harmful lifestyle. Satan is seeking to devour the souls of humanity. The result of sin is death. James 1:15 explains, "Then desire when it has conceived gives birth to sin, and sin, when it is fully grown, brings forth death." Further, Romans 5:12 declares the sober truth, "Therefore, just as sin came into the world through one man, and death through sin, and so death spread to all men because all sinned." Satan is not a bad friend or a mean-spirited boss or a hypocritical parent; Satan is a killer, a murderer. The devil wants to corrupt every soul in the world. Satan is an assassin.

Mountain Goat Assassins

And now this chapter has come full circle: Why do I hate, yes hate, mountain goats? Because these filthy beasts have kicked down untold amounts of deadly rocks on me while climbing the Colorado 14,000-foot mountains. The worst I experienced was during one trip to the famous Maroon Bells and Pyramid Peak. These mountains are considered class four climbing because of the steep terrain.

When hiking through the numerous gullies, the mountain goats are higher than me, and the goats would start jumping around and kicking down large rocks. The rocks pick up incredible speed because of the steep mountainside. The trail through the gullies is narrow and steep and there is no way to avoid the rocks raining down. I had nothing but fervent prayer protecting me from these deadly projectiles. Even though I had a helmet on to protect my head, one hit from a stone would have thumped me off the side of the mountain to a grisly death after a long fall.

On that day, we discovered that the only way to stop the goats was to pee. As it turns out, the salt in urine tastes just as good to them as the salt from a peanut. So our group alternated relieving ourselves on the slope to give us sufficient opportunity to get farther down. Once the rocks started flying again, someone else had to do a number one to stop the trained killers from jumping around. When people see mountain goats, they see cute; I see death staring me straight in the face.

Sadly, people have been fooled by both mountain goats

and sin. People see evil as fun, entertaining, pleasurable, and exciting. For a time, that is true for sin, but in the end, it always leads to death and destruction. In Christ, people counteract the consequences of sin through life.

> Let not sin therefore reign in your mortal body, to make you obey its passions. Do not present your members to sin as instruments for unrighteousness, but present yourselves to God as those who have been brought from death to life, and your members to God as instruments for righteousness. For sin will have no dominion over you, since you are not under law but grace (Rom 6:12–14).

While I am currently the lone member of the Death to Mountain Goats Club, I must be somewhat right about them because Satan has been portrayed as a goat through much of history. Through the years, Satan has been pictured with horns, hooves, and goat-like features. During the medieval age, the image started to gain popularity. A magazine called *Fast Company* did an article on Satan's changing face throughout the centuries. The article noticed that the devil looked more like a goat in the 1500s, but his face has transformed into more of a human form today. Instead of the creepy goat man, Satan has started to look like a human. The goal of Satan is coming to life. He is making sin look safe and fun, and people are falling for his deadly trap.

Questions

1. What keeps us from seeing the utter horror and darkness of sin?

2. How would we be blessed to better grasp that horror and darkness?
3. Explore the impact and implications of "Sin is always cloaked."
4. Why do people still seem to think that they can hide their sin from God?
5. Chapter 8 offers a list of ways to fight sin. What would you add to that list?

Chapter 9

Time, Talent, Treasure

Components of a Hero's Journey

J oseph Campbell wrote a book called *The Hero with a Thousand Faces* in which he analyzes the classic stages of the hero's journey and discusses what all heroes face on the pathway to success. People have used his insights to create various renditions of the hero's journey for decades.

The journey begins with an ordinary person living an ordinary life. There is nothing special about the individual, nothing that would set him apart as a hero versus an average citizen.

Then the hero is called to an adventure. During this initial adventure, the hero finds a mentor, someone who comes beside him to prepare him for the journey's next leg. While in this stage, the hero realizes that there are tests, allies, and enemies. He or she must learn to discern the differences between those who hinder and those who help.

It is at this point that the hero faces the main ordeal, and the challenge becomes more intense. The hero must rise to the challenge or fail. When victory is secured, the hero is rewarded with honor and privilege, but an internal change has also happened to him. After the pressure and test, the hero looks to share his victory as a changed individual. The tests and trials that the hero has endured have transformed him for eternity. The hero has acquired the scars and insight that no one but experience can teach him; he has a new understanding that can help everyone around him.

Mentorship

Think about all the stories that follow this pattern in modern movie-making. There is Katniss, who meets Haymitch; Luke Skywalker and Obi-Wan Kenobi; Neo, and Morpheus; and even Frodo has Gandalf. The newer Marvel movies have Iron Man playing the role of mentor to Spiderman's journey. The journey starts with a person facing a call to action and someone coming alongside to help him or her on the trip. There is knowledge or wisdom that an older hero has that is passed on to the future hero. The cycle continues to move within a circle because heroes are formed and then they in turn produce new heroes. The point of transformation is more significant than gaining fame or success or wealth. It is when the hero becomes the mentor and finds his ultimate purpose in reproducing himself within others by sharing what he has gained.

Too often within Christianity, heroes are created but fail to impart the secrets of success to a successor. Think about congregations that had famous ministers. The minister was part of tremendous growth, but after he leaves, the growth stops and the congregation never recovers from the glory years. The members talk about the past and lose the ability to dream of a brighter future. There are also congregations that have elders who oversee the work that creates impressive good in the community, but the eldership replaces itself with lesser quality men over time and the quality of the congregation slowly diminishes. People start looking elsewhere to be part of the work of the Lord. A true hero's journey does not end with him riding off into the sunset in glory, but rather it ends when he returns with the needed lessons for the next generation to start a new cycle of hero's journeys.

Unselfish Hero

An individual goes on a journey of a wild transformation to then provide that same journey for other people. The entirety of the journey is made to assist the individuals around us. The struggles in the Lord are to shape Christians to be a gift to fellow Christians. God has shown His children important exercises for profound development, endurance, conquering difficulties, and procuring the unspeakable delight of being a loyal servant to the Lord's church. The benefits of the hero's changes should not be limited to one soul, however, they ought to be spread to all.

The apostle Paul went on a hero's journey. He left behind his high standing in Judaism to travel throughout the known world sharing the gospel with the Gentiles. Through his travels, he discovers Barnabas, the Son of Encouragement, as well as countless detractors and enemies seeking to murder or imprison him. He overcomes the challenges of shipwrecks, beatings, imprisonment, and near-constant abuse in the name of Christ. In Acts, he addresses the Ephesian elders as a man who has found the elixir of life. He has accumulated knowledge and wisdom and seeks to impart his knowledge to the leaders of the congregation. Notice his mindset:

Therefore, be alert, remembering that for three years I did not cease night or day to admonish everyone with tears. And now I commend you to God and to the word of his grace, which can build you up and give you the inheritance among all those who are sanctified. I coveted no one's silver or gold or apparel. You yourselves know that these hands ministered to my necessities and to those who were with me. In all things, I have shown you that by working hard in this way, we must help the weak and remember the words of the Lord Jesus, how he said, "It is more blessed to give than to receive" (Acts 20:31–35).

Paul gave of himself to the people in three significant ways. He gave them his time, talent, and treasures. In other words, there is no such thing as a selfish hero.

Treasure

Paul was not greedy (Acts 20:33–35). Instead, he used his resources to minister to others. He worked with his hands to provide for himself. Paul, in these verses, quoted the teaching of Jesus while He was on earth. We do not have a record of Jesus saying, "it is more blessed to give than to receive" within the Gospel accounts, but this wisdom must have been passed on through the years by Christ's followers. One of the reasons that it is more blessed to give than to receive is that you have already been blessed. You have your needs taken care of, you are in a position of strength, and you have a generous heart. The blessing of having trust in the Lord is fantastic because you know that God cares for you in the future and the present. You are refusing to be anxious about the direction of your life. What a fantastic position to be in. You have and you can spread hope.

Talent

Paul admonished and commanded the people how to serve the Lord (Acts 20:31–32). He invested his talent in the people. A hero helps create future heroes by imparting to them the lessons that the hero has learned through his journey. We have shared a lot of Paul's talent through his writings, but think about all of the other insights, lessons, and sermons he delivered to people throughout his life. The word of God's grace being explained by Paul would be captivating.

When Jesus was walking on the Emmaus Road in Luke 24, He was talking with two travelers. The listeners reflected on this conversation in Luke 24:32, "They said to each other, 'Did not our hearts burn within us while he talked to us on the road, while he opened to us the Scriptures?'" Listening to Paul would certainly not be like listening to Jesus speak, but imagine how rewarding it would be. Instead of wishing for your time back, you would have hoped that Paul never ended his speech. Even if Paul were not a great speaker, his insights into the word of Grace would have been mind-blowing.

When someone invests talent in others, the result is the building up of that person. They become stronger through another person's skills. Like a tiny snowball continues to pick up snow as it rolls down a hill, talent has a way of snowballing, continually increasing in size. As the mass of the snowball increases, the capacity of the ball to get more and more snow also increases.

The Proverbs writers understood that intelligence can be shared and can compound. An individual sharing intelligence doesn't diminish his own insight. He instead adds to the student's cleverness. Proverbs 2:7 says, "he stores up sound wisdom for the upright; he is a shield to those who walk in integrity." The idea of sharing wisdom is that the individual sharing has the knowledge already while the individual learning the ability has expanded in wisdom as well. Both individuals are developed through utilizing the gifts of the mentor.

Wisdom is an infinite resource. It is not at all like a limited amount of building blocks in which two individuals are creating peaks, one peak doesn't need to be limited because the other individual's peak is taller. The pinnacles instead increase each other's height. The point of the parable of the talents is that you can multiply talent by using God's gifts to you for the benefit of others (Matt 25:14–30).

Time: The Greatest Gift

Warren Buffett, a famous investor and one of the wealthiest people on earth, once reflected on his life saying that he could buy anything he wanted. He is worth over 80 billion dollars, so a new house or car is nothing to him, but he can never add one second to his life through his wealth. Time is the gift that people give that is most precious. Paul notes in Acts 20:31, "Therefore be alert, remembering that for three years I did not cease night or day to admonish everyone with tears."

Paul stayed with the Christians in Ephesus for three years. Think about what Paul gave the people. If Paul offered you a gift of one of three choices—all of his wealth, for him to teach you a particular talent, or three years' worth of his time—it would be a no-brainer choice. How precious to be in the presence of Paul! His gold would be worthless compared to his time. What people want most is someone else's time.

Time is so valuable that it is the greatest gift you can give to God. God does not need money; He does not require your talents, but your spending time with the Lord is precious to Him. How a person uses time is also an indication of spiritual maturity. Ephesians 5:16 says, to make "the best use of the time, because the days are evil." Time wasted is a life wasted. Everyone has watched a movie that was so bad that they wished they had their two hours back. The plot made no sense, and the special effects were not very special. The movie ended, and instead of feeling satisfied or entertained, you felt terrible because you could have been doing so much more with your time than watching that pointless movie. Maybe even in the first thirty minutes, you realized that the movie was bad, yet instead of turning it off, you continued watching. You were optimistic. "It must improve at some point," but it didn't. Any time that you feel you need your hour back, you have fallen into the trap of sitting around idly.

No one can add minutes to life, but you can control how you use the minutes you have. In Ephesians 5:16, the first phrase can mean to "redeem the time." The word "redeem" can mean "to buy back." To redeem creates an image in your mind, and as Paul says, you own your time. It is yours to use. You can waste time or use time. The best way to use time is to always fit in the crucial elements of your life. Putting God first, making family a priority, and enjoying life are all priority time uses. But watching Netflix, overeating, or mindlessly searching the internet will all have you wishing you had your hours back. Never let the secondary drown out the most important.

Many people go on a hero's journey to accomplish a grand goal, but the end goal is to return and give back to the people. What is your hero's journey? Keep in mind that responding to this question isn't sufficient. You have not completed the course until you come back with something that will bless others on their journey. People often think about what to accomplish but rarely think about what to give back after their transformation. The wilderness will change you, so step out of the desert with a blessing and a commitment to give to others.

Questions

1. In what ways can it be helpful to think of our own walk with God as "a hero's journey"?
2. In what ways must we be careful as we employ language like "a hero's journey" to describe our walk with God?
3. Explore the statement: "Spiritually speaking, everyone can be someone's hero."
4. Explore the statement: "God blesses us so that we can bless others."
5. How can we enhance our practice of mentoring other Christians?

Chapter 10

Light, Leaven, Life
Christ Flows Through Us

B etween sets on the bench press, I was making small talk with a young man about making gains. We both shared the same desire to increase the amount of weight we could bench press at one time, which is called maxing out. This is natural talk for men at the gym as going over the 200-pound number is a high status symbol. But eventually the conversation turned away from weightlifting to weightier matters. He asked me what I did for a living, and I asked him, which is another small talk ritual. I told him I was a minister at a local church of Christ, and he stated that he worked in a local factory. The name of the factory was familiar to me because one of my elders was the manager there. He ran the entire place, and I engaged in a little name dropping to brag just a little. I believed that he, as a factory worker, would be impressed that his highest-level boss was part of our congregation and the high quality of our congregation would be established. I believed wrong.

Instead, the young man gave me a stunned look of contempt. He was astounded to learn that his boss, my elder, was a Christian. I'll never forget his next words. He said, "That man is the biggest liar and cheat I have ever known. I cannot believe he is a Christian." So much for making a good impression for the congregation and myself. The fellow weightlifter was shocked to hear that his boss was a Christian, and I was equally surprised to hear that my elder was acting like a heathen.

No one can entirely control his or her influence on others. Even Jesus couldn't control people's free will around Him. Some people rejected Him, even calling Him a drunkard, while other people embraced Him. Influence is uncertain, but its fluctuating nature should not provide an excuse to ignore a Christian's duty to be a light in the world. A Christian's influence is powerful in a world of darkness. Each follower of Christ is equally responsible for representing the ideals taught by Christ and mentoring his/her brethren on the right path.

Jesus was adamant that believers should guard against misusing their influence. For example, He provided a stern rebuke for those who would influence children negatively, especially where it led them to sin:

> Whoever receives one such child in my name receives me, but whoever causes one of these little ones who believe in me to sin, it would be better for him to have a great millstone fastened around his neck and to be drowned in the depth of the sea (Matt 18:5–6).

Use Your Influence Wisely

Influence has the power to be destructive or constructive. The image of the millstone drives home the severity of poor guidance. Christ's audience would understand the millstone's weight and size, knowing that it could weigh between a few dozen pounds to a few hundred pounds.[1] Jesus's admonishment is a grave warning that fortifies the significance of directing our kids down the path of light. If we don't, we share in their wrongdoings. We should not use our influence flippantly without considering who we are influencing. We should use our influence to have a godly effect on others. Thinking only of ourselves makes us blind to the possible repercussions stemming from our actions. An individualistic perspective ignores others' needs and Christ's most important lesson: To love and guide one another toward salvation.

We are all light, leaven, and life as we share our lives with the world. How we use our influence will speak volumes to the world around us about the nature of Christ. Often, people in the church are hyper-concerned with the effect that the world is having on them and/or their children. There is almost an assumption that influence from the world is evil and that all Christians are automatically light and leaven that bless others.

What is more common is that the world and the church misunderstand one another. Both sides are suspicious of one another, and neither side trusts the other. The world believes that the majority of Christians are judgmental, hate gay people, and are self-righteous. At the same time, church people see the world as selfish, materialistic, and misdirected. Both sides see the other through stained glass presumptions. The church and the world are intent on managing the influence of the other party. Christians are vigilant in protecting themselves from the world, and the world has become increasingly militaristic about guarding against the inroads of Christian morals.

No Christian can be perfect in influence, but all Christians can grow in their stewardship of influence. There will always be people like the Pharisees who will reject Christianity, but countless sinners will gravitate toward people who offer acceptance and love like Jesus. It seems today that sinners run from Christians while in the first century, the sinner was undeniably attracted to Christ and His teachings.

Salt and Light

Jesus used metaphors to illustrate the use of influence in Matthew 5. The first image is tasteless salt.

> You are the salt of the earth, but if salt has lost its taste, how shall its saltiness be restored? It is no longer good for anything except to be thrown out and trampled under people's feet (Matt 5:13).

Jesus's concern is for those Christians who have not been transformed; people in the church acting like the world or even worse. They have not developed the fruit of the Spirit enough to be salt that adds to a bland meal. A healthy, transformed Christian adds joy, love, peace, patience, and understanding to a relationship. Even if people disagreed with the tenets of a Christian's faith, the average person should gain respect for them and enjoy being around them and their Christ-centered attitude.

When Charity and I first got married, we were still adjusting to one another. Charity was the cook in the family, raised by a long line of fantastic cooks, and I was raised within a family that prepared whatever I felt like for supper. In other words, I was a little too picky. If my mother cooked a meal we did not like, we had the option to make something else for ourselves. My mother would not cook it, but we could throw whatever we could find into the toaster oven.

One evening Charity prepared a casserole with peas, some mac and cheese, and a few other foods. I remember telling her that this was not my favorite, and she got pretty upset. With just a few words, it was communicated that I had better eat what was set before me. Out of respect, I began eating the casserole. It was terrible. It was like eating salt straight from the shaker. I ate as much, as I could but when I had enough, I spoke up again, which resulted in another talk, and back to the fork I went. When Charity sat down to enjoy the meal she had prepared, she took one bite and spat it out. She had put way too much salt in the food.

Pouring too much salt into food creates a disgusting, inedible dish. Sometimes Christians throw too much salt on people. Instead of being respectful of differences of opinion within a postmodern world, Christians come off as smug or arrogant. No one feels a sense of sweet honesty and a loving spirit instead they feel judged and condemned through words and body language. There is a sweet spot of saltiness that creates wonderful things such as salted caramel, and everyone loves a good potato chip. But no one likes a salt packet.

The second metaphor Jesus used in Matthew 5 is light.

You are the light of the world. A city set on a hill cannot be hidden. Nor do people light a lamp and put it under a basket, but on a stand, and it gives light to all in the house. In the same way, let your light shine before others, so that they may see your good works and give glory to your Father who is in heaven (Matt 5:14–16).

Like salt, light can be overpowering too.

We love having light. Stumbling around in a dark room looking for the light switch is frustrating, especially if there are Legos on the floor. And walking on a path without a headlamp is treacherous. But when someone shines a bright flashlight directly in your face, it's annoying.

Individuals seldom reflect on the destructive part of the light, because in most scenarios light is a gift. But too much-focused light at one time is damaging; that is why shining a laser at someone's eyes can be blinding—permanently. Before iPhones and smartphone cameras had flashes, people used massive flash bulbs attached to the top of their cameras. If the sky or room were a tad bit dark, the flash would go off and blind everyone for a few seconds. That much light hurt people's eyes. And one should never look directly into the sun. The light overwhelms the ability of the eyes to take it all in, and too much light is damaging to the body

To be a Christian influence for good is a blessing to those around you. A light on a hill is like a lighthouse. No seafarer ever cursed a lighthouse. The lighthouse is appreciated because it is helpful. It's the same with a light in a dark room. A little lamp burning gave a nice glow to light the area during the ancient days. The light was a precious blessing for those who were enslaved in the dark. If people are not finding you to be a blessing in their lives, you might not be acting like Christ around them. Being argumentative and combative rarely creates a positive impression of Christianity.

Leaven

Like salt and light, leaven can also corrupt the entire cause. Paul warns the Corinthians of leaven's influence, saying,

> Your boasting is not good. Do you not know that a little leaven leavens the whole lump? Cleanse out the old leaven that you may be a new lump, as you are unleavened. For Christ, our Passover lamb, has been sacrificed. Let us therefore celebrate the festival, not with the old leaven, the leaven of malice and evil, but with the unleavened bread of sincerity and truth (1 Cor 5:6–8).

Paul is dealing with the destructive influence of sexual sin in Corinth. A man is having an affair with his stepmother, and the congregation refuses to remove the man. Allowing sinful behavior increases the likelihood of the sin becoming justified. Like the mustard seed principle, a little good can go a long way, and the opposite is that a bit of evil can spread rapidly. Influence in either direction is powerful.

Imagine if you could see all the influence you have had over a lifetime and all the kind words that inspired people during downtrodden times. Unlike the movie *It's a Wonderful Life*, not all people have influenced this world for the good. All people influence for good or evil. Let's say you meet someone and make a bad decision to try a narcotic together. When you come down from the high you realize how damaging that behavior is, clean up your life, and never contact them again. But the other person, since that one night, never stopped until he died from an overdose. You could watch a movie called *It's a Horrible Life* about the effects of your wicked friend doing bad deeds and how many lives his influence affected in a negative way.

What might your impact resemble in this world? We need to spend the rest of our lives making strides toward good. Leaven goes a long way, so watch your influence. Paul explains this principle to Timothy: "Keep a close watch on yourself and the teaching. Persist in this, for by so doing you will save both yourself and your hearers" (1 Tim 4:16). Your actions can save you and those around you or condemn you all. Your positive example of Christian living, commitment to the truth, and wisdom in situations can all help prepare someone else for a more robust faith in Christ.

Life

When people think about Jesus Christ, many thoughts come to mind. He was the Son of God. He was perfect. He was all-powerful and could read the hearts of humankind. He healed people. He loved people. But one element that must never be overlooked is that He lived *with* humanity. He did not come to rule *over* humanity. He slept in the same house with His apostles, shared the same food, and walked on the same dusty roads as His friends. He spent time with people. Of all of the glorious theological truths in the book of John, it tells of an important truth,

> In the beginning was the Word, and the Word was with God, and the Word was God. He was at the beginning with God. All things were made through him, and without him was not anything made that was made. In him was life, and the life was the light of men. The light

shines in the darkness, and the darkness has not overcome
it (John 1:1–5).

This passage shows us a God who is so powerful that He
created the earth and a God who is so transcendent that He
has always existed. He is the same God who laughed with
humanity. He was one of the guys, one of us.

The incarnation concept is so majestic that we sometimes forget that it means that He "camped" with us. He sat
around a fire, told stories, shared snacks, and laughed and
joked and played. He was a God that was there, fully
present, enjoying relationships and people. The goal of
transformation is to connect with others and allow them to
feel the blessings of someone who has taken on the characteristics of Christ. For those people around us to feel loved,
respected, and encouraged. How do people feel around you?
Are you a blessing to them or a draining force? Love well
because Christ loved with all of His life.

There is one player on my tennis team. I call him Justin,
but not because his name is Justin. His real name is Lucas. I
call him Justin because he is the Justin Timberlake of the
team, and we are his backup singers. I use it as a way to
pump him up for a match. I'm there to help him look great.
The championship one year came down to a troublesome
season finisher match. His opponent was a skilled player
who had beaten him once before earlier in the season. It was
a must-win game. At the end of it, he triumphed over his
opponent. On the way back home, we turned on some
NSYNC and listened to "Bye, Bye, Bye." We laughed, we
talked, and that song will stay with him. It was about sharing
a moment and rejoicing in a win together. His parents
divorced; he never saw his dad, so the connection was trans-

formative. Over the years, I have sung Taylor Swift songs, Sheryl Crow songs, and Vanilla Ice songs with friends and kids. It was more than fun. It was a celebration of climbing a mountain, winning a tennis match, or any other victory. It was sharing a life.

Questions

1. How does God honor us by letting us be light, leaven, and life in this sin-damaged world?
2. What are the dangers of excessive salt and light in the process of evangelism and spiritual transformation?
3. Who has blessed—or is blessing—you as salt, light, and leaven? Do they know how important they are to you?
4. In what sense was Jesus "one of the guys" with His disciples? In what ways do we need to be careful with this statement?
5. How can we increase the impact of our roles as salt, light, and leaven for both the lost and our brethren?

Endnotes

[1] Wilkins, Michael J. *Matthew,* Zondervan Illustrated Bible Backgrounds Commentary, Clinton E. Arnold, ed. (Grand Rapids: Zondervan, 2002), 113.

Chapter 11

Read, Reflect, Restore

Take Time to Let God In

Admiral William H. McRaven, a Navy SEAL, wrote a book titled *Make Your Bed*. The book is based on a graduation speech he gave in 2014 to the graduating class from the University of Texas. In the preface of the book he says the book was based on "the ten lessons I learned from Navy SEAL training ... ten lessons that were important in dealing with the challenges of life." Here is an excerpt from the first lesson.

> The bed was as simple as the room, nothing but a steel frame and a single mattress. A bottom sheet covered the mattress, and over that was a top sheet. A gray wool blanket tucked tightly under the mattress provided warmth from the cool San Diego evenings. A second blanket was expertly folded into a rectangle at the foot of the bed. A single pillow, made by the Lighthouse for the Blind, was centered at the top of the bed and intersected at a ninety-degree angle with the blanket at the bottom. This was the standard. Any deviation from this exacting

requirement would be cause for me to "hit the surf" and then roll around on the beach until I was covered head to toe with wet sand—referred to as a "sugar cookie."

Standing motionless, I could see the instructor out of the corner of my eye. He wearily looked at my bed. Bending over, he checked the hospital corners and then surveyed the blanket and the pillow to ensure they were correctly aligned. Then, reaching into his pocket, he pulled out a quarter and flipped it into the air several times to ensure I knew the final test of the bed was coming. With one final flip the quarter flew high into the air and came down on the mattress with a light bounce. It jumped several inches off the bed, high enough for the instructor to catch it in his hand.

Swinging around to face me, the instructor looked me in the eye and nodded. He never said a word. Making my bed correctly was not going to be an opportunity for praise. It was expected of me.[1]

Just like the Navy SEALS were expected to make their bed every morning, Christians are expected to read the Bible. It is one of the essential practices of a Christ-follower. The discipline is a fundamental habit that all other habits build on. No one can become more like Christ without first reading about Christ. Studying and applying Scripture is a core behavior that multiplies the other spiritual practices.

Reading the Word of God is a watershed behavior. A watershed moment is a crucial dividing point for a person. Scripture provides a stable foundation for Christianity. As soon as someone denies the inspiration of Scripture and rejects the Bible's authority, everything else becomes chaotic. Jesus is the basis of faith, but no one would ever find that faith without the Bible. Since we are not eyewitnesses of Christ, we need scripture to show us, Christ. John 20:30–31 says,

> Now Jesus did many other signs in the presence of the disciples, which are not written in this book; but these are written so that you may believe that Jesus is the Christ, the Son of God, and that by believing you may have life in his name.

Reading or hearing scripture was a precious practice in ancient times. All books were copied by hand and were expensive to own, so only the wealthy had books. The ordinary people longed for the opportunity to hear the Word of God read aloud and to have God's wisdom imparted to them. Too often in America, people read the Bible to have God join them in life. The person is self-centered instead of Scripture-centered. We do not read the Bible to find out how to get God into our lives; instead, we read so that we will join God in His life. There is a radical difference between asking, "What does this Scripture mean to me?" and asking, "What is God telling me to do?" We search for more than mere meaning; we look to obey. The question is not "who is my neighbor?" It is "Will I be a neighbor?"

Spreading the Word Meaningfully

The Bible has become so commonplace in America that numerous copies of Scripture will sit dormant on bookshelves for years without being read. An individual can pull up ancient and sacred writing on their cell phone, read the holy text in different versions, and even lose track of a copy of the Bible with little concern. Overexposure to sacred text has made underexposure change.

Notice the attitude that individuals had toward holy text in the Old Testament. Ezra comprehended the motivation behind the sacred text. "For Ezra had set his heart to study the Law of the Lord, and to do it and to teach his statutes and rules in Israel" (Ezra 7:10). Ezra was intentional, and he set his heart and studied; not for mere knowledge, but to do what was asked of him. He obeyed. Finally, he realized that Scripture is to be shared, so he spread it to others. Coming in contact with divine communication has to prompt more than a warm feeling. Scripture creates initiative to act.

Over the last decade, there has been an effort to replace biblical-focused study with a nebulous spirituality. A standard line is that members of the Lord's church are too concentrated on the Bible and not on the Christ of the Bible. Of course, the Bible is the communication from God, not a replacement for God. A person is not saved by the Bible nor matured through Bible study alone. A classic tale is told of a person who spends all of his or her time pouring over love letters and ignoring the person who wrote them. But Jesus and the Bible are not at odds with one another. Rather they complement one another. The choice is not either Jesus or the Bible, but instead, one is so in love with Christ that he desires to listen to everything that Jesus says. Put it this way, "If you love me, you will keep my commandments" (John 14:15). The words of God sustain the relationship. Matthew 4:4 adds, "But is written, 'Man shall not live by bread alone, but by every word that comes from the mouth of God.'"

Adopting a Spiritual Point of View

A man on one side of a river shouts to a man standing on the other side, "Hey, how do I get to the other side of the river?" The other man responds, "You are on the other side of the river." This is funny because it violates a skill so essential in social interaction that you take it almost entirely for granted. When talking to another person, you have to adopt that person's point of view.[2] Too often in Bible reading, we are on the other side of the river wanting Jesus to come to us, but the role of scripture is for us to get on God's side. He does not want to join you in your life. He is commanding you to join Him in His life. The Bible reorients a person's worldview and defines reality. Too often, people infuse culture and current concerns into the Bible. To read the Bible is to enter into a realm between heaven and earth.

Orienting Yourself with the Bible

In the reading of Scripture, a sense of dislocation is prevalent. A person becomes disoriented because the Bible upends the wisdom of the world. Bible reading has to be paired with reflection. Reflection defines the significance of what we are reading.

To reflect is to see current events and modern problems through the lens of godliness. One is viewing the scripture through God's perspective. One might have ears, but do those ears hear what is God genuinely saying? If the Good Samaritan's famous story took place today, a western lady would hesitate to help, pondering the safety of aiding the outsider. A money manager would be worried about the time that helping will take because time is money. A mom might worry about the impact on her children. A teen will view the parable through the lens of one's ability to afford the help needed and what they should even do. Instead of reading the parable with a lens of God, people read scripture through culturally shaded glasses. Reflection uses time and thought to remove modern or cultural concerns and allow the essence of biblical authority to flow into the reader's mind.

Reflection can be a private discipline but also can be rewarding within a community. One congregation that I know of read Matthew 10 for ten weeks straight. The group would come together on Wednesday nights to examine the scripture. The minister told me he was amazed at the insight and interconnections that the group saw through the intentional study. Perhaps in the past, the common practice of the church was to read through a book of the Bible with someone declaring for all the hearers "it means what it means and says what it says." That is true, but maybe there is more. Only reflection can parse the deeper meanings, and through review, people can see what God wants us all to see in His inspired word. God is needing us to be in alignment with His interests and command. Second Timothy 2:15 says, "Do your best to present yourself to God as one approved, a worker who has no need to be ashamed, rightly handling the word of truth."

Reflection Makes Us Who We Are

The ability to reflect separates us from all other animals. No monkey has probably ever reevaluated how he ate a banana. In one study, analysts looked at the intellectual capacity of 105 two-year-olds compared to that of 106 adult chimpanzees, using tests including both actual objects and social items.

The first set of tests involved tracking where food was located after it had been hidden or moved, being able to choose and then use the correct tool to get food otherwise out of reach, and being able to use sound as a cue for the location of a hidden reward (such as the sound of food rolling around inside a cup).

In the tests involving social items, another part of the mind was affected. These social tests included being able to solve a problem correctly after watching the experimenter solve it, and being able to use an experimenter's gaze as a hint to where food was located (this required understanding that where a person is looking is a cue for what he or she is thinking), and using a person's unsuccessful attempt to open a canister as an indication that there was food inside it.

The results were both clear and profound. When completing the physical tests, the kids and chimps were neck and neck: both solved 68 percent of the problems correctly. But when completing the social difficulties, where another part of the mind was involved, the kids trounced the chimps, with 74 percent to 36 percent accuracy. Our species has conquered the earth because of our ability to understand others' minds, not because of our opposable thumbs or handiness with tools.[3] The ability to learn from one another, and to process Scripture together, allows a more profound reflection for all parties involved. After reading and reflecting on the inspired Bible, the next step is to restore God's ideal reality to earth.

Mirroring God's Vision

People who criticize a restoration desire see the feeling of patterns as an action in and of itself. Individuals are looking to re-establish the first-century church in today's church. However, that is a limited perspective on the longing to recreate the example of the New Testament. In the wake of perusing the Bible, the hope is to reestablish God's optimal vision of the world.

Throughout the Bible, there is a restoration theme. In Genesis, there is the tree of life, which was forbidden from eating. But because the man ate of the tree, he introduced sin into the world. In Revelation, there is the restoration of humanity having access to the tree of life. God seeks to restore that which is broken. The reading of scripture helps produce a world that restores the ideals of the Lord. A person views scripture as what God would have His creation to be. The Bible is more than information; it is the invitation for transformation. In reading the Bible, change or restoration is not a goal, vision, or wish; it is the basic experience of a Christian.

Questions

1. Why would any Christian neglect or shortchange Bible reading?
2. How can we encourage respectful, reflective Bible reading within the church? Our families?
3. In what ways is reflecting on a biblical text different from—and superior to—imposing our opinions on that text?

4. In what ways is Bible reading and reflection on the text spiritually transformative? How does it bring us closer to the mind and heart of Jesus?

5. To what degree and under what conditions can immersion in Scripture help us learn to see life as God sees it?

Endnotes

[1] McRaven, Admiral William H. *Make Your Bed: Little Things That Can Change Your Life ... and Maybe the World* (New York: Grand Central Publishing, 2017), 11–12.

[2] Epley, Nicholas. *Mindwise: How We Understand What Others Think, Believe, Feel, and Want* (New York: Knopf, 2014), 86.

[3] Epley, *Mindwise*, 86.

[4] Epley, *Mindwise*, 86.

Chapter 12

Faith, Hope, Love

Components of a Virtuous Life

I n Thirsty for God" A Brief History of Spirituality, Bradley P. Holt uses a story that is told by Anthony De Mello. It is a powerful illustration of having the ability to discern that which is most valuable. Value is often assigned, but rarely understood.

> A monk in his travels found a precious stone and kept it. One day he met a traveler, and when he opened his bag to share his provisions with him, the traveler saw the jewel and asked the monk to give it to him. The monk did so readily. The traveler departed overjoyed with the unexpected gift of the precious stone that was enough to provide him with wealth and security for the rest of his life. However, a few days later, he came back in search of the monk, found him, gave him the stone, and implored him: "Now give me something much more precious than this stone, valuable as it is. Give me that which enabled you to give it to me."[1]

The man realized that there was something even more precious than a stone full of security. The ability to give away an item of such immense value was indeed what was most wanted. The man acknowledged there was something more important than material belongings. He needed to find out about the center of genuine change. He needed to find out how somebody who was God could leave the wonders of paradise and come to earth. He needed to find out how to be an individual who could forfeit his potential wealthy life for others' welfare. Being a person of this magnitude of character was a precious blessing far more valuable than a stone ensuring privilege and power. True freedom and power are something more profound than what a mere gem could buy.

Answers Are Hard to Find

Finding the source of the ability to give away the gem is a pursuit for the ages. We are part of a culture in which electronics can give us the answer to any question we ask. At the touch of our fingers, a computer screen will be filled with pages of answers and even predetermines the "best" answers and places them on the first page. But rarely does anyone click on page two of these answers. The ability to seek the truth is rare. We become impatient when the "real" world demands effort and time to search for answers when we can get a million hits on Google in .16 seconds.

Real searching, the kind Jesus assures us will result in finding, is too taxing. Searching for truth is hard. Jeremiah 29:13 declares, "You will seek me and find me when you seek me with all your heart." Jesus states in Matthew 7:7, "Ask, and it will be given to you; seek, and you will find; knock, and it will be opened to you." To understand real transformation and experience a radical change, one must search diligently for the truth. And that means to search for the truth, not to have the right answers or appear intelligent, but rather to understand the secrets to fulfillment.

While being skinned alive, one Christian in India looked at his persecutors and said, "I thank you for this. Tear off my old garment, for I will soon put on Christ's garment of righteousness."[2] Genuine change is developing to a point where confidence, expectation, and love are more significant than abundance, force, and advantage. Having the trifecta of otherworldly qualities is a definitive objective in our wild changes. How can modern Christians find what is most precious?

Finding Transformation

Paul provides the values that transform a life. In his famous chapter on love, he gives the three keys to sanctified living.

> Love never ends. As for prophecies, they will pass away; as for tongues, they will cease; as for knowledge, it will pass away. For we know in part and prophesy in part, but when the perfect comes, the partial will pass away. When I was a child, I spoke like a child, I thought like a child, I reasoned like a child. When I became a man, I gave up childish ways. For now, we see in a mirror dimly, but then face to face. Now I know in part; then I shall know fully, even as I have been fully known. So now faith, hope, and love abide, these three; but the greatest of these is love (1 Cor. 13:8–13).

Imagine a life that is wholly engrossed in faith, hope, and

love. Think about the aroma that would emanate from a Christian that has been so bathed in these virtues. The spirit of Christ would be a sweet fragrance coming from him or her.

Faith

There is no better definition for faith than Hebrews 11:1, "Now faith is the assurance of things hoped for, the conviction of things not seen." The idea of faith being an assured conviction of a believable truth is vital. A person's truth is the promises of God. The concept of faith is more profound than intellectual assent, instead, moves to a reality that creates actions. James 2:14 explains, "What good is it, my brothers, if someone says he has faith but does not have works? Can that faith save him?" A person of strong faith has a security that is unlike any material resource. No one can take a person's faith away from him or her. In contrast to natural fortune or even connections that can be wrecked, faith is a lasting installation. Belief in Jesus is an anchor for the storms of life.

One sees the power of faith during tragedy and struggles. The resolve a person has in the face of suffering is a testament to one's dedication. There is a deep-seated trust in the assurances of God. Strong faith is built on more than facts. Too often, people believe that faith merely understands the truths of the gospel. The more that someone knows *about* God is equated with *knowing* God. All the details of spirituality or Christianity are not automatic faith builders. A person can memorize the Bible and spit back entire genealogies from the Old Testament but fall apart during uncertain times in life.

Faith is seen when there is nothing to see. To create strong faith, the essential elements of the gospel have to be shared. Paul in 1 Corinthians 15:1–3 summarizes the gospel by highlighting the three core truths of Christ—He has died for our sins, was buried, and was raised from the dead. A God who could do that is the God that can be trusted when all looks bleak and dark. Minutia rarely creates massive change. The core elements of the gospel are what Christians stand on during hard times.

The human mind focuses on significant shifts and emotional details more than small facts. There was an experiment in which someone was shown a picture of a complicated situation—in one case, a group of people in a subway car. The car appears to be an Eighth Avenue Express. There are various advertisements posted on the vehicle, and five people are seated, including a rabbi and a mother carrying her baby. But the focus of the picture is two men arguing. They are standing up, and one is pointing at the other and holding a knife.

A mock game of telephone starts. The first person (transmitter) is asked to describe the picture to someone else (receiver) who cannot see it. The transmitter then leaves the room, and a new person enters. That new individual turns into the receiver. The first recipient turns into the transmitter, sharing what occurred in the picture with the new receiver, who has not seen the image. The game is rehashed to a fourth, fifth, and in the long run sixth individual. Individuals analyzing that experiment looked at which story subtleties were passed along the transmission chain. They found that the amount of data shared dropped significantly each time the story was shared. Around 70% of the story subtleties were lost in the initial five to six transmissions.

The reports did not just become shorter: they were also sharpened around the essential details. In the story about the subway car, the first person telling the tale mentioned all the details. They talked about how the subway car seemed to be an Eighth Avenue Express. But as the story was passed down the telephone line, many unimportant details were dropped. People stopped talking about what type of subway it was or where it was traveling and instead focused on the argument —the fact that one person was pointing at the other and brandishing a knife. The significant shifts in the story show how the details are forgotten.

The gospel's core elements need to be emphasized over remembering the small details to build strong faith.

Hope

The idea of hope has turned into the concept of optimism, but hope is more significant than positive thinking. Hope is having a crystal-clear view of the future. Paul mentions this fact: "For now we see in a mirror dimly, but then face to face. Now I know in part; then I shall know fully, even as I have been fully known" (1 Cor 13:12). In talking to the readers of his letter, Paul tells them that in contrast to the spiritual gifts that seem so valuable, hope is much more certain to come to fruition. The struggle with hope is the ability to see into the future. No one can see what will happen in the future besides God. Humans see the future through a dark room, using our best predictive abilities to guess what will happen in the end. Throughout time humans have been wrong about what will happen in the coming years. Hope is the trust that what God says will occur. Rather than investigating a broken mirror, Christians, through expectation, see eye to eye the truth that God has guaranteed. Christians know, not guess, what will happen at the end of time.

The Hebrews writer defines the pursuit of hope for all Christians.

> Though we speak in this way, yet in your case, beloved, we feel sure of better things—things that belong to salvation. For God is not unjust so as to overlook your work and the love you have shown for his name in serving the saints, as you still do. And we desire each one of you to show the same earnestness to have the full assurance of hope until the end, so that you may not be sluggish, but imitators of those who through faith and patience inherit the promises (Heb 6:9–12).

Hope is like a game show. There are different choices to pick from. One door has a vehicle, while other doors have small, unimportant prizes. Several of the entries are empty. There would be massive frustration over the pick. Yet, not at all like a game show of possibility, the Christian knows without question the prize that God has guaranteed for the unwavering individuals. The assurance of this hope provides unspeakable confidence to embrace life while on earth. A better reward is waiting for the believer on the other side of time.

Love

There is no real spiritual transformation worth mentioning without love being the central aspect of a changed life. Paul highlights the greatness of love in 1 Corinthians 13:13, "So now faith, hope, and love abide, these three; but the greatest of these is love." Maybe it sounds trite to talk about love being the prominent attribute of spiritual formation because everyone who has an ounce of scriptural knowledge is not shocked that love is at the forefront. But regardless of the common accusation of being too simple, love is first for all Christians.

John states in 1 John 4:7–8,

> Beloved, let us love one another, for love is from God, and whoever loves has been born of God and knows God. Anyone who does not love does not know God because God is love.

Of all the attributes that John could have mentioned, such as compassion, kindness, tolerance, patience, or forgiveness, he says that love is the highest defining characteristic of a Christian.

Even Paul in Galatians 5:22 notes that love is central. "But the fruit of the Spirit is love, joy, peace, patience, kindness, goodness, faithfulness, gentleness, self-control." In this sentence, people usually read that the Spirit's fruit is plural but notice that the sentence has a singular verb. He uses the word "is" and then mentions "love." He could be saying the fruit of the Spirit is love and then defining what love looks like through the other qualities. Love is a permanent attribute of Christianity. The Bible speaks of God being love. It is not something that He does, but something that defines Him. A man is flesh, not that he acts like flesh; he is flesh. A truly transformed Christian does not act loving or choose to be loving on certain occasions; he is loving because he is defined by love. A Christian could no more stop being loving as God could stop being loving. Love is truly the highest level of transformation because it changes an individual into a caring person. The quality of love never ends. Once people have been perfected through love, this quality stays with them throughout eternity. Unlike hope and faith that will no longer be needed in the afterlife, love never passes away, because how could it? Perfected love is complete. The perfected Christian is love.

Love is the answer to how the man can give away his precious gem. Love is the root of his actions. An example of this is found in *Les Misérables*. One night, Jean Valjean shows up at a priest's door, asking for a place to stay the night. Bienvenu graciously loves him, feeds him, and gives him a bed. But Valjean steals most of Bienvenu's silver and runs off in the night. The police capture Valjean and return him to confront Bienvenu. At the point when the lawmen speak to Bienvenu, they have discovered the silver in Valjean's backpack; Bienvenu amazingly tells the police that he had offered them to Valjean as a blessing. He reprimands Valjean for not accepting the silver candles too. After the law leaves, Bienvenu tells Valjean to use the silver to become an honest man. A man can only accomplish an act like this by developing a character saturated with love. A mature Christian is love, not just loving.

Questions

1. Explain the famous adage; "To give is to love; to love is to give."
2. In what ways does Scripture challenge us to give like God gives?

3. Why to many continue to prefer blind optimism or the power of positive thinking when God so clearly offers Christ as our hope?

4. Faith grows as we
   _____.

5. In what ways to trouble and struggle offer special opportunities for growing in faith?

Endnotes

[1] Holt, Bradley P., *Thirsty for God: A Brief History of Christian Spirituality* (Minneapolis: Fortress Press, 2017), 250–251.

[2] Platt, David, *Radical: Taking Back Your Faith from the American Dream* (Colorado Springs: Multnomah Books, 2010), 35.

[3] Berger, Jonah, *Contagious: Why Things Catch On* (New York: Simon & Schuster, 2016), 199–200.

Chapter 13

Conclusion

Spiritual formation is a journey, not a destination. But the journey is not linear, it is wild. Spiritual transformation is full of surprises, disappointments, and victories. One thing that spiritual transformation is not is tame.

You are at the end of this book, but really just the beginning of your journey with Christ. You have come this far, where will you go from here? What is so exciting about spiritual maturity is the directions that you can take. There are probably areas of weakness in your walk with the one who walked on water. There are also areas of spiritual strength. You have gifts that can be used to bless the world around you. Hopefully, a chapter or two jumped out at you. Something that got you stirred up to focus on for the future.

One of my elders recently shared with me a note on his phone. It appeared at the beginning of every day. It was his reminder to read the Bible. When I preached these lessons to the congregation, the lesson on reading and reflecting jumped out to him. He said he "always knew he needed to read, but the way that I put reading that day made a lasting impression." It was his moment of conviction to do something new. Maybe after reading this book, you will have that one area that you cannot settle in any longer. You know you have to change. Do not put down this book without making one spiritual commitment to go on that wild journey of transformation with the Lord. Conquer that one sin, start that one habit, invest in that one person. You might fail or you might succeed. That is just part of the process. Whatever improvement you make, whatever step you take, it will increase your spiritual maturity. You will not get there instantly, but you owe it to yourself to try.

Let me leave you with this story. I was watching this show called *Alone*. The premise of the show was that individuals were taken out to the wilderness to survive for as long as possible by themselves. No cell phones, no fast food, and no other people. You had to find your own food and provide your own shelter. The area was in the northern part of Canada on the West coast. There were plenty of bears in the area. One person on the show named Desmond was from Atlanta. Before he was dropped off, one of the producers of the show asked him, "What will you do about the black bears?" Desmond looked at the camera and said, "If there is a bear fight, you better check on the bear." Sadly, Desmond did not make it one night in the wild because he was scared when he saw bear scat. Hopefully, Christians are more action than talk.

We need to have real confidence. Set your mind to the goal of growing in Christ. If there is someone that is going to be strong in Christ, you be it. If all of the world is compromising, you stand firm. If there is a bear fight, you better check on the bear because you will be fine. Go get this. Be wild.

Questions

1. How does it bless us to know that the journey of spiritual transformation "is not linear; it is wild"?

2. As used above, what does "wild" mean? What must it NOT mean?

3. In what ways do you see Wild Transformation blessing your spiritual growth? What must happen for those blessings to become reality?

4. Which chapter in Wild Transformation has proven most challenging for you? Why?

5. What makes seeking to know Christ Jesus life's most challenging and most rewarding adventure?

Scripture Index

1 Timothy

2:4	64–65
2:9	37
4:16	95
6:11	76

2 Timothy

2:3	54
2:15	103

Titus

2:14	33

Hebrews

4:15	58
5:8–9	48
6:9–12	113
10:24–25	15–16
11:1	110
13:17	43

James

1:2–4	53
1:5	14
1:14–15	73
1:15	76
1:21	63
2:14	110

1 Peter

1:16	27
2:13	43
2:20–24	55–56
5:3	46

1 John

1:5–10	63
4:7–8	114

Revelation

2:10	54–55

Credits

Also By Cypress Publications

Always Near: Listening for Lessons from God
by Bill Bagents

Approaching Christian Scripture Faithfully: Twenty Attempts
by Ed Gallagher

The Christian Life: Chapters for Bible Teacher
by Ed Gallagher

Cruciform Christ: 52 Reflections on the Gospel of Mark
by Travis Bookout

Easing Life's Hurts 2nd ed.
by Jack Wilhelm and Bill Bagents

Equipping the Saints: A Practical Study of Ephesians 4:11–16
by Bill Bagents and Cory Collins

The Holy Spirit: A Bible Study Guide
by Jack Wilhelm

Jesus the Christ: Chapters for Bible Teachers
by Ed Gallagher

King of Glory: 52 Reflections on the Gospel of John
by Travis Bookout

Rescue: God and Sin in the Old Testament
by John F. Wakefield

Revisiting Life's Oases: Soul-Soothing Stories

by Bill Bagents

Romans: A Practical Commentary

by Brian Poe

Welcoming God's Word: Reading with Head and Heart

by Bill Bagents

*WHAM! Facing Life's Heavy Hits: Thirteen Old Testament
Encounters*

by Bill and Laura S. Bagents

*WHAM! Facing Life's Heavy Hits: Thirteen New Testament
Encounters*

by Bill and Laura S. Bagents

Women in the Shadows

by Betty Hamblen

CYPRESS

To see full catalog of Heritage Christian University Press
and its imprint Cypress Publications, visit
www.hcu.edu/publications

www.ingramcontent.com/pod-product-compliance
Lightning Source LLC
Chambersburg PA
CBHW050442150626
46551CB00028B/1157